Talk To Me In Korean
Workbook
Level 2

written & designed by
Talk To Me In Korean

Talk To Me In Korean Workbook (Level 2)

1판 1쇄 · 1st edition published	2013. 10. 14.
1판 18쇄 · 18th edition published	2023. 1. 30.

지은이 · Written by	Talk To Me In Korean
책임편집 · Edited by	선경화 Kyung-hwa Sun, 스테파니 베이츠 Stephanie Bates
디자인 · Designed by	선윤아 Yoona Sun
삽화 · Illustrations by	장성원 Sungwon Jang
녹음 · Voice Recordings by	선경화 Kyung-hwa Sun
펴낸곳 · Published by	롱테일북스 Longtail Books
펴낸이 · Publisher	이수영 Su Young Lee
편집 · Copy-edited by	김보경 Florence Kim
주소 · Address	04033 서울특별시 마포구 양화로 113, 3층(서교동, 순흥빌딩) 롱테일북스
	3rd Floor, 113 Yanghwa-ro, Mapo-gu, Seoul, KOREA
이메일 · E-mail	TTMIK@longtailbooks.co.kr
ISBN	978-89-5605-689-0 14710

*이 교재의 내용을 사전 허가 없이 전재하거나 복제할 경우 법적인 제재를 받게 됨을 알려 드립니다.

*잘못된 책은 구입하신 서점이나 본사에서 교환해 드립니다.

*정가는 표지에 표시되어 있습니다.

TTMIK - TALK TO ME IN KOREAN

Talk To Me In Korean Workbook
Level 2

Contents

How to Use
the Talk To Me In Korean Workbook

This workbook is designed to be used in conjunction with the Talk To Me In Korean Level 2 lessons, which are available as both a paperback book and an online course at TalkToMeInKorean.com. Developed by certified teachers to help you review and reinforce what you've learned in the Talk To Me In Korean lessons, this workbook contains 3 main categories of review and 10

Categories

1. Vocabulary
2. Comprehension
3. Dictation

Types of Exercises

1. Matching
2. Crossword puzzle
3. Multiple choice

4. Translation
(Korean<->English)
5. Short answer
6. Define and translate
7. Fill in the chart
8. Fill in the blank
9. True/False
10. Q&A

The "Dictation" category was designed to aid in the development of Korean listening skills. When you come across the "Dictation" category, you will listen to an audio file of a word or phrase in Korean and write down what you hear. The "Dictation" audio files are available for download in MP3 format at https://talktomeinkorean.com/audio.

Romanizations are provided, but we encourage you to refer to our "Quick Guide to 한글 (Han-geul)" to help you learn how to read and write in 한글 (Han-geul). Only relying on romanizations hinders your learning and actually prevents you from becoming better at Korean. So, do yourself a favor and learn 한글 (Han-geul) if you haven't already.

Quick Guide To 한글 (Hangeul)

The Korean alphabet is called 한글 (Hangeul), and there are 24 basic letters and digraphs in 한글.
*digraph: pair of characters used to make one sound (phoneme)

Of the letters, fourteen are consonants (자음), and five of them are doubled to form the five

tense consonants (쌍자음).

Consonants

Basic

ㄱ	ㄴ	ㄷ	ㄹ	ㅁ	ㅂ	ㅅ	ㅇ	ㅈ	ㅊ	ㅋ	ㅌ	ㅍ	ㅎ
g/k	n	d/t	r/l	m	b/p	s	ng	j	ch	k	t	p	h
g/k	n	d/t	r/l	m	b/p	s/ɕ	ŋ	dʑ/tɕ	tɕʰ	k/kʰ	t/tʰ	p/pʰ	h

Tense

ㄲ	ㄸ	ㅃ	ㅆ	ㅉ
kk	tt	pp	ss	jj
k'	t'	p'	s'	c'

When it comes to vowels (모음), there are 10 basic letters. 11 additional letters can be created

by combining certain basic letters to make a total of 21 vowels. Of the vowels, eight are single

pure vowels, also known as monophthongs (단모음), and 13 are diphthongs (이중모음), or two

vowel sounds joined into one syllable which creates one sound.

*When saying a monophthong, you are producing one pure vowel with no tongue movement.

*When saying a diphthong, you are producing one sound by saying two vowels. Therefore, your

tongue and mouth move quickly from one letter to another (glide or slide) to create a single

sound.

Vowels

Monophthongs

ㅏ	ㅓ	ㅗ	ㅜ	ㅡ	ㅣ	ㅐ	ㅔ
a	eo	o	u	eu	i	ae	e
a/aː	ʌ/əː	o/oː	u/uː	ɨ/ɯː	i/iː	ɛ/ɛː	e/eː

Diphthongs

ㅑ	ㅕ	ㅛ	ㅠ		ㅒ	ㅖ
ya	yeo	yo	yu		yae	ye
ja	jʌ	jo	ju		jɛ	je

ㅘ	ㅝ				ㅙ	ㅞ
wa	wo				wae	we
wa	wʌ/wəː				wɛ	we

					ㅚ	ㅟ	ㅢ
					oe	wi	ui
					we	wi	ɨi

* Please refer to the book "한글마스터(Hangeul Master)" for more information.

Writing 한글 letters

한글 is written top to bottom, left to right. For example:

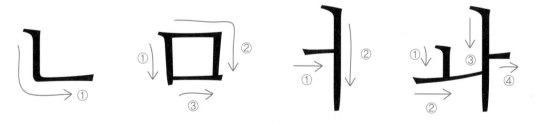

By making sure you follow the stroke order rules, you will find that writing Korean is quite easy and other people will be able to better read your handwriting.

Syllable Blocks

Each Korean syllable is written in a way that forms a block-like shape, with each letter inside the block forming a sound/syllable.

In each syllable block, there is a:

1. * Beginning consonant

2. * Middle vowel

3. Optional final consonant

* Required in a syllable block. A block MUST contain a minimum of two letters: 1 consonant and 1 vowel.

ㅊ + ㅣ + ㄴ (ch+i+n) = chin

ㄱ + ㅜ (g+u) = gu

친 (chin) + 구 (gu) = 친구 (chingu) = "friend"

Two of the most common ways to write consonant and vowel combinations in Korean are horizontally and vertically (the boxes drawn here are for illustrative purpose only).

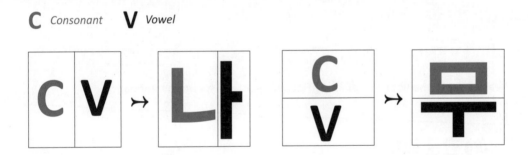

By adding a final consonant (받침), the blocks are modified:

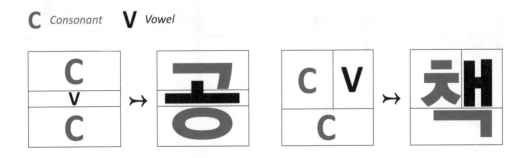

There are also syllables which have two final consonants, such as:

In all the syllable blocks, the letters are either compressed or stretched to keep the size relatively the same as the other letters.

Vowels

Since the "minimum two letter" rule exists and one letter has to be a consonant and the other has to be a vowel, what can you do when a vowel needs to be written in its own syllable block? Add the consonant ㅇ [ng] in front of or on top of the vowel. When reading a vowel, such as 아, the ㅇ makes no sound and you just pronounce the ㅏ [a].

Vowels absolutely, cannot, under any circumstances be written by themselves!!

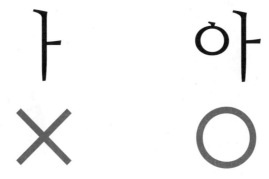

Okay! Now that you are equipped with a basic knowledge of 한글,
it's time to do your part and start practicing!
Let's get to it!

Lesson 1.
Future Tense -ㄹ/을 거예요

Section I – Vocabulary

Please define and translate each word in English. Then write it in your pre-ferred language.

1. **가다**
   [ga-da]
   _____

2. **하다**
   [ha-da]
   _____

3. **입다**
   [ip-da]
   _____

4. **만나다**
   [man-na-da]
   _____

5. **팔다**
   [pal-da]
   _____

6. **언제**
   [eon-je]
   _____

7. **어디**
   [eo-di]
   _____

8. **지금**
   [ji-geum]
   _____

9. 내일
   [nae-il]
   _____

10. 얼마
    [eol-ma]
    _____

11. 이거
    [i-geo]
    _____

12. 티셔츠
    [ti-syeo-cheu]
    _____

13. 청바지
    [cheong-ba-ji]
    _____

14. 혼자
    [hon-ja]
    _____

Section II - Comprehension

True/False – Decide if the statement is true or false. If it is false, correct the underlined term or phrase so that the statement is true.

15. 뭐 할 거예요? = What are you doing?
    [mwo hal geo-ye-yo?]

    ››

16. Verb stems ending with a vowel, such as 보다 and 가다, are followed
    [bo-da]   [ga-da]

by 르 거예요.
   [l geo-ye-yo]

    ››

17. Verb stems ending with a consonant, such as 먹다 and 입다, are followed
[meok-da]   [ip-da]
by ㄹ 거예요.
[l geo-ye-yo]

   »

18. "Where are you going to meet?" = 어디에서 팔 거예요?
[eo-di-e-seo pal geo-ye-yo?]

   »

19. The most common way of making future tense sentences in Korean is by
adding ㄹ/을 거예요.
[l/eul geo-ye-yo]

   »

20. When verbs are changed into the future tense, they take on the meaning
of "to be going to do [something]," or "will do [something.]"

   »

Section III - Writing

In Korean, write a response to the question using a complete sentence and the prompt in parenthesis.

Ex.
누구 만날 거예요? (Kyeong-eun)
[nu-gu man-nal geo-ye-yo?]

Answer : 경은 씨 만날 거예요.
[gyeong-eun ssi man-nal geo-ye-yo.]

21. 언제 할 거예요? (tomorrow)
[eon-je hal geo-ye-yo?]

Answer :

22. 뭐 먹을 거예요? (samgyeopsal; Korean barbecue)
[mwo meo-geul geo-ye-yo?]

Answer :

23. 그 가방 얼마에 팔 거예요? (5,500 won)
[geu ga-bang eol-ma-e pal geo-ye-yo?]

Answer :

Section IV - Dictation

Listen to the corresponding MP3 file. Repeat aloud what you hear, then write it down. Each word/phrase will be said twice.

24. Track 1:

25. Track 2:

Lesson 2.
Object Marking Particles
을, 를

Section I – Vocabulary

Fill in the chart – An example has been provided. In the last column, please use your preferred language.

Word	Part of speech (noun, verb, adverb, adjective)	English translation from dictionary or TTMIK	Sentence, word, or image to help me remember
케이크 (ke-i-keu)	noun	cake	I'm going to eat 케이크 for dessert.
1. 사과 [sa-gwa]			
2. 텔레비전 [tel-le-bi-jeon]			
3. 지갑 [ji-gap]			
4. 왜 [wae]			
5. 이상하다 [i-sang-ha-da]			
6. 자주 [ja-ju]			

Section II - Writing

Write the following words with the correct object marking particle.

7. 밥 (을/를): _____
   [bap]

8. 오렌지 주스 (을/를): _____
   [o-ren-ji ju-seu]

9. 그 사람 (을/를): _____
   [geu sa-ram]

10. 가방 (을/를): _____
    [ga-bang]

11. 고양이 (을/를): _____
    [go-yang-i]

12. 학교 (을/를): _____
    [hak-gyo]

13. 카메라 (을/를): _____
    [ka-me-ra]

14. 커피 (을/를): _____
    [keo-pi]

을/를 or 이/가
[eul/reul]   [i/ga]

Section III - Comprehension

Fill-in-the-blank

Choose either 을/를 or 이/가 to complete each sentence.
           [eul/reul]   [i/ga]

15. 오늘 날씨(   ) 너무 좋아요.
    [o-neul nal-ssi-(   ) neo-mu jo-a-yo.]

    *너무 = too (much); very
    [neo-mu]

16. 자전거(   ) 탈 거예요.
[ja-jeon-geo-(   ) tal geo-ye-yo.]

* 자전거 = bicycle
[ja-jeon-geo]

* 타다 = to ride
[ta-da]

17. 화장실(   ) 어디예요?
[hwa-jang-sil-(   ) eo-di-ye-yo?]

* 화장실 = restroom, bathroom
[hwa-jang-sil]

18. 옷(   ) 예뻐요.
[ot-(   ) ye-ppeo-yo.]

* 옷 = clothes
[ot]

19. 밥(   ) 많이 먹었어요.
[bap-(   ) ma-ni meo-geo-sseo-yo.]

Section IV - Dictation

Listen to the corresponding MP3 file. Repeat aloud what you hear, then write it down. Each word/phrase will be said twice.

20. Track 3:

21. Track 4:

22. Track 5:

Lesson 3.
And, and then, therefore, so
그리고, 그래서

Section I - Vocabulary

Complete the crossword puzzle by writing the English translation for each Korean word in the corresponding spaces.

Across

1. 김치
[gim-chi]

5. 그래서
[geu-rae-seo]

Down

1. 한국 음식
[han-guk eum-sik]

2. 커피
[keo-pi]

8. 그리고
[geu-ri-go]

3. 학생
[hak-saeng]

10. 비가 오다
[bi-ga o-da]

4. 친구
[chin-gu]

11. 집
[jip]

6. 물
[mul]

12. 밥
[bap]

7. 프랑스
[peu-rang-seu]

13. 빵
[ppang]

9. 돈
[don]

Section II - Comprehension

Multiple choice - Circle the best answer.

14. 그래서 means:
   [geu-rae-seo]

   a. Therefore

   b. And

   c. So

   d. both A and C

15. If you want to say "and" or "and then", you would use:

   a. 친구
   [chin-gu]

   b. 만나다
   [man-na-da]

   c. 그거
   [geu-geo]

   d. None of the above

16. What is the Korean word for "conjunction", a word that connects two sentences, clauses, or phrases?

> a. 접속사
> [jeop-sok-sa]
>
> b. 삼겹살
> [sam-gyeop-sal]
>
> c. 현우
> [hyeo-nu]
>
> d. 경은
> [gyeong-eun]

17. "비가 왔어요" is the past tense form of 비가 오다.
[bi-ga wa-sseo-yo]   [bi-ga o-da]

> a. I don't know
>
> b. False
>
> c. Pizza
>
> d. True

18. 김치 많이 먹어요?
[gim-chi ma-ni meo-geo-yo?]

> a. 네! 김치 맛있어요!
> [ne! gim-chi ma-si-sseo-yo!]
>
> b. 아니요.
> [a-ni-yo.]
>
> c. 왜요?!
> [wae-yo?!]
>
> d. I've never eaten it before.

Section III - Reading comprehension

Read the following journal entry. Unless otherwise noted, all words, sentence endings, and tenses have been covered in TTMIK Levels 1 and 2. Based on what you read, answer the questions below in English.

> * 내다 = to pay
> [nae-da]

2013-7-31

오늘 현우 씨를 만났어요. 그리고 밥을 먹었어요. 저는 돈이 없었어요. 그래서
[o-neul hyeo-nu ssi-reul man-na-sseo-yo. geu-ri-go ba-beul meo-geo-sseo-yo. jeo-neun do-ni eop-sseo-sseo-yo. geu-rae-seo

현우 씨가 돈을 냈어요. 그리고 커피숍에 갔어요. 커피숍에서 저는 물을 마셨
hyeo-nu ssi-ga do-neul nae-sseo-yo. geu-ri-go keo-pi-syo-be ga-sseo-yo. keo-pi-syo-be-seo jeo-neun mu-reul ma-syeo

어요. 그리고 현우 씨는 커피를 마셨어요.
-sseo yo. geu-ri-go hyeo-nu ssi-neun keo-pi-reul ma-syeo-sseo-yo.]

19. Who did this person meet today?

→

20. Who paid for the meal?

→

21. Why did the person pay?

→

22. Where did they go after having a meal?

→

23. What did the writer have to drink?

→

Section IV - Dictation

Listen to the corresponding MP3 file. Repeat aloud what you hear, then write it down. Each word/phrase will be said twice.

24. Track 6:

25. Track 7:

26. Track 8:

Lesson 4
And, with 하고, (이)랑

Section I – Vocabulary

Match each Korean word to its common English translation.

1. 매운 (adjective form of 맵다)
   [mae-un]

   a. sweet

2. 번개
   [beon-gae]

   b. to eat

3. 사다리
   [sa-da-ri]

   c. Gyeongbok Palace

4. 춤을 추다
   [chu-meul chu-da]

   d. to dance

5. 대통령
   [dae-tong-ryeong]

   e. spicy

6. 단 (adjective form of 달다)
   [dan]

   f. President

7. 선생님
   [seon-saeng-nim]

   g. ladder

8. 경복궁
   [gyeong-bok-gung]

   h. teacher

9. 먹다
   [meok-da]

   i. lightning

10. 좋아하다
[jo-a-ha-da]

                                     j. movie, film

11. 영화
[yeong-hwa]

                                     k. to like

12. 천둥
[cheon-dung]

                                     l. to be scared, to be scary

13. 무섭다
[mu-seop-da]

                                     m. thunder

Section II - Comprehension

Short answer - Please respond to the following questions in English. Then write the answer in your preferred language to help you remember.

14. Why do you add the suffix -씨 to someone's name when speaking in 존댓말?
[-ssi]   [jon-daen-mal]

15. How do you know whether to use 이랑 or 랑?
[i-rang]   [rang]

16. What is the difference between 하고 and 그리고?
[ha-go]   [geu-ri-go]

17. 하고 and (이)랑 can also mean "with". What word can you add to make it
[ha-go]   [(i)-rang]
super clear that you actually mean "together with" instead of "and"? Write a
sentence using this addition.

Section III - Dictation
Listen to the corresponding MP3 file. Repeat aloud what you
hear, then write it down. Each word/phrase will be said twice.

18. Track 9:

19. Track 10:

20. Track 11:

Lesson 5.
Days of the Week 요일

Section I - Vocabulary

Choose a word or words from the "Word Bank" to best complete each sentence.
Not all words are used.

Word Bank

밤 [bam]	영화를 보다 [yeong-hwa-reul bo-da]	수 [su]
화성 [hwa-seong]	언어 [eo-neo]	목 [mok]
소풍을 가다 [so-pung-eul ga-da]	요일 [yo-il]	금 [geum]
소풍 [so-pung]	화 [hwa]	토 [to]
영화 [yeong-hwa]	월 [wol]	일 [il]

1.   (   ) stands for "earth", "soil", or "ground".

2.   I'd like to learn a new (   ), maybe Farsi.

3.   Would you like to go on a (   ) today? I will bring the food!

4. (   ) is "Thursday" in Korean.

5. Let's go shopping at (   ) when it's really dark outside.

6. "To watch a movie" in Korean is (   ).

7. "Mars" in Korean is (   ).

8. (   ) stands for "tree".

Section II - Comprehension: Yesterday and Tomorrow

Fill in the chart - The first one has been done for you as an example.

어제 [eo-je]	오늘 [o-neul]	내일 [nae-il]
Ex. 월요일 [wo-ryo-il]	화요일 [hwa-yo-il]	수요일 [su-yo-il]
9.	토요일 [to-yo-il]	10.
11.	목요일 [mo-gyo-il]	12.

13.	일요일 [i-ryo-il]	14.	
15.	수요일 [su-yo-il]	16.	
17.	금요일 [geu-myo-il]	18.	
19.	월요일 [wo-ryo-il]	20.	

Section III - Dictation

Listen to the corresponding MP3 file. Repeat aloud what you hear, then write it down. Each word/phrase will be said twice.

21. Track 12:

22. Track 13:

23. Track 14:

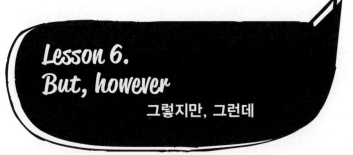

Lesson 6.
But, however
그렇지만, 그런데

Section I – Vocabulary

Please define/translate each word in English. Then write it in your preferred language.

1. **피곤하다:**
   [pi-go-na-da]
   _____

2. **영화:**
   [yeong-hwa]
   _____

3. **학교:**
   [hak-kkyo]
   _____

4. **일요일:**
   [i-ryo-il]
   _____

5. **일어나다:**
   [i-reo-na-da]
   _____

6. **매일:**
   [mae-il]
   _____

7. **어젯밤:**
   [eo-jet-ppam]
   _____

8. **살이 빠지다:**
   [sa-ri ppa-ji-da]
   _____

9. **늦게:**
[neut-ge]
_____

10. **말짱하다:**
[mal-jjang-ha-da]
_____

Section II - Writing practice

Write each syllable or word on the lines to practice your handwriting skills. Saying the syllables and the words aloud as you
write them in the spaces below will help you learn faster!

11. **그**
[geu]
————— ————— ————— ————— —————

12. **럳**
[reot]
————— ————— ————— ————— —————

13. **지**
[ji]
————— ————— ————— ————— —————

14. **만**
[man]
————— ————— ————— ————— —————

15. **런**
[reon]
————— ————— ————— ————— —————

16. **데**
[de]
————— ————— ————— ————— —————

17. **그렇지만**
[geu-reo-chi-man]

_____ _____ _____

18. **그런데**
[geu-reon-de]

_____ _____ _____

> 그런데 or 그렇지만
> [geu-reon-de] [geu-reo-chi-man]

Section III - Comprehension

Use either 그런데 or 그렇지만 to fill in the blanks.
[geu-reon-de] [geu-reo-chi-man]

19. ( ) is used more in everyday conversations than
( ).

20. ( ) is used to contrast two facts and express
that the resulting discovery is disappointing.

21. ( ) means "but" or "and", depending on the
context.

Section IV - Dictation

Listen to the corresponding MP3 file. Repeat aloud what you hear, then write it down. Each word/phrase will be said twice.

22. Track 15:

23. Track 16:

24. Track 17:

Lesson 7.   −한테, −한테서
"to [someone]", "from [someone]"

Section I – Vocabulary

Multiple choice – Circle the best answer.

1. The English translation for 누구 is:
    [nu-gu]

    a. me

    b. from

    c. to

    d. who/whom

2. How do you say "friend" in Korean?

    a. 친구
       [chin-gu]
    b. 저
       [jeo]
    c. 진국
       [jin-guk]
    d. 없다
       [eop-da]

3. 맞다 means:
    [mat-da]

    a. generally

    b. to be correct

    c. to translate

    d. to block

4. What does 옷 translate to in English?
   [ot]

   a. rain

   b. above/top

   c. to smile

   d. clothes

5. "From Seoul to Busan" translates to (   ) in Korean:

   a. 서울에게 부산한테
      [seo-u-re-ge bu-sa-nan-te]
   b. 서울한테 부산한테
      [seo-u-ran-te bu-sa-nan-te]
   c. 서울에서 부산까지
      [seo-u-re-seo bu-san-kka-ji]
   d. 서울한테 부산까지
      [seo-u-ran-te bu-san-kka-ji]

Section II - Comprehension

True/False - Decide if the statement is true or false. If it is false, correct the underlined term or phrase so that the statement is true.

6. -한테 and -에게 have the same characteristics, but -한테 is mainly used
   [-han-te]   [-e-ge]   [-han-te]
in written language.

   ››

7. You can only use -한테 and -한테서 about people or animals.
                  [-han-te]   [-han-te-seo]

   ››

8. –한테 has two meanings; "to [someone]" and "from [someone]".
    [-han-te]

    ≫

9. –한테서 and –한테 are always interchangeable.
    [-han-te-seo]   [-han-te]

    ≫

10. "A한테 맞다" can be translated to English as "to get corrected by A".
    [A-han-te mat-da]

    ≫

Section III - Reading comprehension

Read the following journal entry. Unless otherwise noted, all words, sentence endings, and tenses have been covered in TTMIK Levels 1 and 2. Based on what you read, answer the questions below in English.

* 배 = stomach, belly
  [bae]

* 전화를 받다 = to answer a phone call
  [jeo-nwa-reul bat-da]

* 내리다 = to get off; leave
  [nae-ri-da]

* 한 is the adjective form of 하나.
  [han]   [ha-na]

* 도와주다 = to help; to aid
  [do-wa-ju-da]

* 아주머니 = middle-aged woman
  [a-ju-meo-ni]

* 병원 = hospital
  [byeong-won]

오늘 아침 지하철에서 배가 아팠어요. 그래서 친구한테 전화를 했어요.
[o-neul a-chim ji-ha-cheo-re-seo bae-ga a-pa-sseo-yo. geu-rae-seo chin-gu-han-te jeo-nwa-reul hae-sseo-yo.

그런데 친구가 전화를 받지 않았어요. 지하철에서 내렸어요. 사람들한테
geu-reon-de chin-gu-ga jeo-nwa-reul bat-ji a-na-sseo-yo. ji-ha-cheo-re-seo nae-ryeo-sseo-yo. sa-ram-deu-ran-te

말했어요. "도와주세요!" 한 아주머니가 도와줬어요. 그래서 병원에 갔어요.
ma-rae-sseo-yo. "do-wa-ju-se-yo!" han a-ju-meo-ni-ga do-wa-jwo-sseo-yo. geu-rae-seo byeong-wo-ne ga-sseo-yo.]

11. What happened to this person on the subway?

→

12. Who did this person call?

→

13. What did this person do after she got off the subway?

→

14. Who helped this person?

→

15. Where did this person go in the end?

→

Section IV - Dictation

Listen to the corresponding MP3 file. Repeat aloud what you hear, then write it down. Each word/phrase will be said twice.

16. Track 18:

17. Track 19:

18. Track 20:

Lesson 8.
Telling Time
한 시, 두 시, 세 시, 네 시, ..

Section I - Reviewing Korean Numbers

Part I - Match the native Korean number to the Western Arabic equivalent.

1. 여섯
[yeo-seot]

2. 하나
[ha-na]

3. 일곱
[il-gop]

4. 둘
[dul]

5. 여덟
[yeo-deol]

6. 셋
[set]

7. 아홉
[a-hop]

8. 넷
[net]

9. 열
[yeol]

10. 다섯
[da-seot]

11. 열하나
[yeo-ra-na]

12. 열둘
[yeol-dul]

a. 1

b. 2

c. 3

d. 4

e. 5

f. 6

g. 7

h. 8

i. 9

j. 10

k. 11

l. 12

Part 2 - Match each Western Arabic number to the Sino-Korean equivalent.

13. 50

14. 1

15. 2

16. 3

17. 30

18. 4

19. 5

20. 6

21. 7

22. 8

23. 9

24. 10

m. 오
[o]

n. 일
[il]

o. 칠
[chil]

p. 이
[i]

q. 팔
[pal]

r. 삼
[sam]

s. 구
[gu]

t. 사
[sa]

u. 십
[sip]

v. 오십
[o-sip]

w. 삼십
[sam-sip]

x. 육
[yuk]

Section II - Comprehension

Write each time in Korean as if you were answering the question "지금 몇 시 몇 분이에요?" Say the time aloud.
[ji-geum myeot si myeot bu-ni-e-yo?]

* Only hours are marked in Native Korean.

25.
_____

26.
_____

27.
_____

28.
_____

8:57 PM

4:19 AM

29. _____

30. _____

Section III - Dictation
Listen to the corresponding MP3 file. Please write your answer using an Arabic numeral (1,2,3,4,5...etc.) Each word/ phrase will be said twice.

31. Track 21:

32. Track 22:

33. Track 23:

Lesson 9.
Counters 개, 명

Section I – Vocabulary
Translate each word to Korean. Then write it in your preferred language.

1. pencil =

2. stone =

3. ball =

4. kimchi stew =

5. To be left; to remain =

6. duck =

7. candy =

8. how many (things) =

9. bag =

10. cat =

11. apple =

12. hamburger =

13. coffee =

14. paper =

15. person =

Section II - Comprehension

Write the appropriate Korean counter for each word.

16. People/person: _____

17. Animals: _____

18. Things: _____

19. Bottles: _____

20. Books: _____

21. Papers/tickets/pages: _____

22. Cars, punches: _____

Section III - Translation Practice
Translate the following to Korean:

23. Fifteen apples =

24. Nine cats =

25. Twenty-two sheets of paper =

26. Five books =

27. Thirty pencils =

28. Please give me one book. =

29. There are eleven dogs. =

Talk To Me In Korean Workbook

Section IV - Dictation

Listen to the corresponding MP3 file. Repeat aloud what you hear, then write it down. Each word/phrase will be said twice.

30. Track 24:

31. Track 25:

32. Track 26:

Lesson 10.
Present Progressive
-고 있어요

Section I - Vocabulary (Verbs)

Please define each word in English and your preferred language.

1. 하다:
    [ha-da]
    _____

2. 보다:
    [bo-da]
    _____

3. 오다:
    [o-da]
    _____

4. 사다 :
    [sa-da]
    _____

5. 듣다:
    [deut-da]
    _____

6. 비가 오다:
    [bi-ga o-da]
    _____

7. 공부하다:
    [gong-bu-ha-da]
    _____

8. 일하다:
    [i-ra-da]
    _____

9. 운동하다:
    [un-dong-ha-da]
    _____

10. **노래하다:**
[no-rae-ha-da]

_____

Section II - Fill in the chart: Progressive verbs

Conjugate the verbs from the Vocabulary section into present progressive verbs, past progressive, and future progressive. An example has been provided.

Infinitive (dictionary form)	Present progressive	Past progressive (past continuous)	Future progressive
Ex. 팔다 [pal-da]	팔고 있어요 [pal-go i-sseo-yo]	팔고 있었어요 [pal-go i-sseo-sseo-yo]	팔고 있을 거예요 [pal-go i-sseul geo-ye-yo]
1a.			
2a.			
3a.			
4a.			
5a.			
6a.			
7a.			
8a.			

9a.			
10a.			

Section III - Comprehension

Short answer - Use English and your preferred language to answer the following question:

11. What are the 2 main things to remember when using present progressive tense in Korean?

Section IV - Dictation

Listen to the corresponding MP3 file. Repeat aloud what you hear, then write it down. Each word/phrase will be said twice.

12. Track 27:

13. Track 28:

14. Track 29:

Lesson 11.
Self-introduction
자기소개

Section I - Vocabulary

Fill in the chart - In the "Translation/Definition" column, use English and your preferred language (if not English). In the "Use it in a sentence" column, please use Korean only.

Word	Translation/Definition	Use it in a sentence (Korean)
1. 수영 [su-yeong]		
2. 중국어 [jung-gu-geo]		
3. 이름 [i-reum]		
4. 선생님 [seon-saeng-nim]		
5. 미국 [mi-guk]		
6. 은행 [eu-naeng]		
7. 여동생 [yeo-dong-saeng]		
8. 초등학생 [cho-deung-hak-saeng]		

9. **중학생** [jung-hak-saeng]		
10. **고등학생** [go-deung-hak-saeng]		
11. **대학생** [dae-hak-saeng]		
12. **취미** [chwi-mi]		
13. **나이** [na-i]		
14. **직장** [jik-jang]		
15. **직업/하는 일** [ji-geop]/ [ha-neun il]		
16. **사는 곳** [sa-neun got]		
17. **가족** [ga-jok]		
18. **친척** [chin-cheok]		
19. **명함** [myeong-ham]		
20. **가르치다** [ga-reu-chi-da]		
21. **태어나다** [tae-eo-na-da]		
22. **살다** [sal-da]		

Section II - Comprehension

Write your own 자기소개 [ja-gi-so-gae] by filling in the blanks with words that are true about yourself!

23. 안녕하세요. 제 이름은 (   )예요/이에요.
[an-nyeong-ha-se-yo.] [je i-reu-meun (   )ye-yo/i-e-yo.]

24. 저는 (   ) 살이에요. 그리고 (   )에 살아요.
[jeo-neun (   ) sa-ri-e-yo.]   [geu-ri-go (   )e sa-ra-yo.]

25. 저는 (   )예요/이에요. (occupation)
[jeo-neun (   )ye-yo/i-e-yo.]

26. 그리고 지금 (   )을/를 공부하고 있어요.
[geu-ri-go ji-geum (   )eul/reul gong-bu-ha-go i-sseo-yo.]

27. 저는 취미가 (   )예요/이에요.
[jeo-neun chwi-mi-ga (   )ye-yo/i-e-yo.]

Section III - Dictation

Listen to the corresponding MP3 file. Repeat aloud what you hear, then write it down. Each word/phrase will be said twice.

28. Track 30:

29. Track 31:

30. Track 32:

Lesson 12. "What is the Date?"

날짜

Section I - Vocabulary

Match each month to its corresponding Korean name. If your preferred language is not English, please translate the English names of the months into your preferred language and write it next to the English word to help you remember more efficiently.

Examples: June/Junio, December/Dicembre

1. December

2. February

3. October

4. April

5. August

6. June

7. July

8. May

9. September

10. March

11. November

12. January

a. 5월
[o-wol]

b. 1월
[i-rwol]

c. 11월
[si-bi-rwol]

d. 6월
[yu-wol]

e. 10월
[si-wol]

f. 2월
[i-wol]

g. 9월
[gu-wol]

h. 8월
[pa-rwol]

i. 7월
[chi-rwol]

j. 3월
[sa-mwol]

k. 12월
[si-bi-wol]

l. 4월
[sa-wol]

Section II - Comprehension

Answer the following questions based on the information found on the calendar.

			5월			
일	월	화	수	목	금	토
			1	2	3	4
5	6	7	8	9	10	⑪ ☆☆ 생일
12	13	14	15	16	17	18
19	20	21	22	23	24 친구 7PM	25
26	27	28	29 meetng 9:30AM	30	31	

* 오전 = AM
  [o-jeon]

* 오후 = PM
  [o-hu]

			6월			
일	월	화	수	목	금	토
						1
2	3	4	5	⑥ 현충일	7	8
9	10	11	12	13	14	15
16	17	18	19	20 ☆휴가☆	21	22
23/30	24	25	26 →	27	28	29

13. What is the date of your birthday?

⟶

14. What month and day does your vacation start?

→

15. What day does your vacation end?

→

16. What date is the Korean holiday of Memorial Day?

→

17. What day and time are you meeting your friend? Also, 몇 월 며칠에 만나요?
[myeot wol myeo-chi-re man-na-yo?]

→

18. What day and time do you have a meeting?

→

Section III - Dictation

Listen to the corresponding MP3 file. Repeat aloud what you hear, then write it down. Each word/phrase will be said twice.

19. Track 33:

20. Track 34:

21. Track 35:

Lesson 13.
Too, also (Part 1) -도

Section I -Vocabulary

Multiple choice - Circle the best answer.

1. The Korean word for "student" is:

    a. 회사
       [hoe-sa]
    b. 학교
       [hak-gyo]
    c. 학생
       [hak-saeng]
    d. 강아지
       [gang-a-ji]

2. When translated to English, 물 is:
       [mul]

    a. water

    b. coffee

    c. cake

    d. hamburger

3. How do you say "please give me" in Korean?

    a. 안녕하세요
       [an-nyeong-ha-se-yo]
    b. 안 해요
       [an hae-yo]
    c. 주세요
       [ju-se-yo]
    d. 일하다
       [i-ra-da]

4. "머리" means:
   [meo-ri]

    a. stomach

    b. head

    c. leg

    d. eye

5. The Korean verb for "to work" is:

    a. 노래하다
      [no-rae-ha-da]

    b. 경화
      [gyeong-hwa]

    c. 물 주세요.
      [mul ju-se-yo.]

    d. 일하다
      [i-ra-da]

6. What is the English translation for the word 오늘?
   [o-neul]

    a. tomorrow

    b. today

    c. yesterday

    d. last week

7. How do you address a middle aged woman or someone who is working in a restaurant who is older than you and married?

    a. 언니
      [eon-ni]

    b. 여동생
      [yeo-dong-saeng]

    c. 여자
      [yeo-ja]

    d. 아줌마
      [a-jum-ma]

8. The Korean word 배 has various meanings. Which of the following is not a
[bae]
translation for 배?
[bae]

   a. boat

   b. pear

   c. stomach

   d. twice

9. The Korean adjective 아프다 means:
[a-peu-da]

   a. to be hurt/to be sick

   b. to be bored

   c. to be awesome

   d. to be stressed

10. How do you say "here" [location] in Korean?

   a. 저기
   [jeo-gi]
   b. 고기
   [go-gi]
   c. 여기
   [yeo-gi]
   d. 이거
   [i-geo]

11. 다른 means:
[da-reun]

   a. everyone

   b. no one

   c. beautiful

   d. another, different, or other

Section II – Comprehension

Fill-in-the-blank

12. 저는도 sounds strange, so in order to use -도, you must get rid of the 는,
   [jeo-neun-do]   [-do]   [neun]

which is known as the (   ).

13. In general, you have to get rid of any (   ) that already

exist there in order to use -도.
                                       [-do]

14. Changing 저 to 나 and dropping the -요 at the end of a sentence turns it
              [jeo]   [na]   [-yo]

into (   ) instead of 존댓말.
                            [jon-daen-mal]

15. -도 modifies different words, so the meaning of the sentence (
   [-do]

).

16. "저도 물 주세요" means (   ).
   ["jeo-do mul ju-se-yo"]

17. "저 물도 주세요" translates to (   ).
   ["jeo mul-do ju-se-yo"]

Section III - Translation Practice
Translate the following to English:

18. 저도 학생이에요.
    [jeo-do hak-saeng-i-e-yo.]

    =

19. 이것도 연필이에요.
    [i-geot-do yeon-pi-ri-e-yo.]

    =

20. 그 사람도 공부하고 있어요.
    [geu sa-ram-do gong-bu-ha-go i-sseo-yo.]

    =

21. 중국도 가고 싶어요.
    [jung-guk-do ga-go si-peo-yo.]

    =

22. 머리도 아파요.
    [meo-ri-do a-pa-yo.]

    =

23. 아줌마~! 여기 콜라 한 병 주세요. 그리고 사이다도 한 병 주세요.
    [a-jum-ma~! yeo-gi kol-la han byeong ju-se-yo. geu-ri-go sa-i-da-do han byeong ju-se-yo.]

    =

Section IV - Dictation

Listen to the corresponding MP3 file. Repeat aloud what you hear, then write it down. Each word/phrase will be said twice.

24. Track 36:

25. Track 37:

26. Track 38:

Lesson 14.
Too, also (Part 2) -도

Section I - Vocabulary

Please define/translate each word in English. Then write it in your preferred language.

1. 영어:
    [yeong-eo]
    _____

2. 가르치다:
    [ga-reu-chi-da]
    _____

3. 컴퓨터:
    [keom-pyu-teo]
    _____

4. 고치다:
    [go-chi-da]
    _____

5. 잡다:
    [jap-da]
    _____

6. 팔다:
    [pal-da]
    _____

7. 사다:
    [sa-da]
    _____

8. 먹다:
    [meok-da]
    _____

9. 보다:
    [bo-da]
    _____

Section II - Comprehension

True/False – Decide if the statement is true or false. If it is false, correct the underlined term or phrase so that the statement is true.

10. In order to construct a sentence using –도 [-do] with verbs, you must use the noun form of the verb + –도 하다. [-do ha-da]

   ❯❯

11. By changing a verb into the noun form, you are literally saying "also + verb in the noun form + to do".

   ❯❯

12. One way to change a verb into a noun is by adding –기 [-gi] to the verb stem.

   ❯❯

13. To use –도 [-do] with a 하다 [ha-da] verb, such as 공부하다, [gong-bu-ha-da] you need to add –기. [-gi]

   ❯❯

14. "저는 매운 음식도 먹어요." [jeo-neun mae-un eum-sik-do meo-geo-yo.] translates to "I eat spicy food as well."

   ❯❯

15. "I even fix computers." is said "컴퓨터를 고치기도 해요." in Korean.
[keom-pyu-teo-reul go-chi-gi-do hae-yo.]

>>

Section III - Dictation

Listen to the corresponding MP3 file. Repeat aloud what you hear, then write it down. Each word/phrase will be said twice.

16. Track 39:

17. Track 40:

18. Track 41:

Lesson 15. Only -만

Section I - Vocabulary

Multiple choice – Circle the best answer.

1. 듣다 means:
    [deut-da]

    a. to write

    b. to listen

    c. to walk

    d. to punch

2. The kinship term 언니 is used by females to address another female who is:
    [eon-ni]

    a. younger

    b. the same age

    c. older

    d. drinking coffee

3. The Korean word for "to come" is:

    a. 오다
       [o-da]

    b. 먹다
       [meok-da]

    c. 놀다
       [nol-da]

    d. 가다
       [ga-da]

4. **책상** is the Korean word for:
   [chaek-ssang]

   a. chair   c. desk

   b. piano   d. platform

5. Translate to English: **일찍**
   [il-jjik]

   a. why   c. today

   b. beer   d. early

6. A **선생님** is a:
   [seon-saeng-nim]

   a. student

   b. teacher

   c. office worker

   d. person who thinks they know everything

7. **놀다** means:
   [nol-da]

   a. to play

   b. to go

   c. to write

   d. to drink

8. If you are watching a **영화**, what are you watching?
   [yeong-hwa]

   a. TV drama

   b. Super Junior concert

   c. movie or film

   d. nothing

9. **아침에** *is what time of day?*
   [a-chi-me]

     a. in the evening

     b. in the morning

     c. in the afternoon

     d. at night

Section II - Comprehension

Fill in the chart - An example has been provided.

Noun or verb	+만	English translation
Ex. 사과 주스 [sa-gwa ju-seu]	사과 주스만 [sa-gwa ju-seu-man]	*only apple juice*
10. 주다 [ju-da]		
11. 일 년 [il nyeon]		
12. 가르치다 [ga-reu-chi-da]		
13. 살다 [sal-da]		
14. 소리 [so-ri]		
15. 여자 [yeo-ja]		
16. 돈 [don]		

17. 소녀시대 [so-nyeo-si-dae]			
18. 읽다 [ik-tta]			
19. 열다 [yeol-da]			
20. 웃다 [ut-da]			

Section III- Dictation

Listen to the corresponding MP3 file. Repeat aloud what you
hear, then write it down. Each word/phrase will be said twice.

21. Track 42:

22. Track 43:

23. Track 44_Ver2:

Lesson 16. A bit, really, very, not really, not at all
조금, 정말, 진짜, 아주, 별로, 전혀

Section I - Vocabulary

Please translate each term to English and make note of any special usages. Then write it in your preferred language.

Example: **별로**: not really, not particularly – always paired with 안 or
[byeol-lo]
a negative sentence structure.

1. **조금**: _____
   [jo-geum]

2. **비싸다**: _____
   [bi-ssa-da]

3. **빠르다**: _____
   [ppa-reu-da]

4. **이상하다**: _____
   [i-sang-ha-da]

5. **정말**: _____
   [jeong-mal]

6. **진짜**: _____
   [jin-jja]

7. **아주**: _____
   [a-ju]

8. **맛있다:** [ma-sit-da]

_____

9. **멀다:** [meol-da]

_____

10. **재미있다:** [jae-mi-it-da]

_____

11. **나쁘다:** [na-ppeu-da]

_____

12. **전혀:** [jeo-nyeo]

_____

13. **바쁘다:** [ba-ppeu-da]

_____

14. **덥다:** [deop-da]

_____

Section II - Comprehension

Please provide short answers to the following questions.

15. As introduced in this lesson, there are multiple ways to say "very". Explain the different usages and degrees of use.

16. **조금** is a noun quantifier, meaning that it is used before a noun to indicate the
[jo-geum]
amount or quantity of something. Explain in what other way you can use this word.

17. What happens to **조금** when pronounced quickly. Can it also be written this
[jo-geum]
way?

18. How are **별로** and **전혀** used in comparison to the other words in this lesson?
[byeol-lo]   [jeo-nyeo]

Section III - Translation practice
Translate the following sentences to Korean.

19. It's a bit expensive. =

20. It's not that expensive. =

21. Hyunwoo is really strange. =

22. This orange is very delicious. =

Section IV- Dictation

Listen to the corresponding MP3 file. Repeat aloud what you hear, then write it down. Each word/phrase will be said twice.

23. Track 45:

24. Track 46:

25. Track 47:

Lesson 17. - (으)ㄹ 수 있다/없다
Can, cannot

Section I - Vocabulary

Complete thc crossword puzzle by writing the English translation for each Korean word in the corresponding spaces.

Across

2. 하다
   [ha-da]

5. 일본어
   [il-bo-neo]

Down

1. 가다
   [ga-da]

2. 운전
   [un-jeon]

8. -(으)ㄹ 수 있다
[-(eu)l su it-da]

3. 읽다
[ik-tta]

9. 자다
[ja-da]

4. -(으)ㄹ 수 없다
[-(eu)l su eop-da]

11. 만나다
[man-na-da]

6. 있다; 존재하다
[it-da]   [jon-jae-ha-da]

7. 보다
[bo-da]

10. 먹다
[meok-da]

Section II - Comprehension

Write an English translation for the following questions. Then answer the questions in Korean using the prompts.

12. 우리 내일 만날 수 있어요? =
[u-ri nae-il man-nal su i-sseo-yo?]

Answer : (네)
[ne]

13. 이 책 읽을 수 있어요? =
[i chaek il-geul su i-sseo-yo?]

Answer : (아니요/못)
[a-ni-yo]   [mot]

14. 떡볶이 만들 수 있어요? =
[tteok-bbo-kki man-deul su i-sseo-yo?]

Answer : (아니요/못)
[a-ni-yo]   [mot]

15. **한국어 할 수 있어요?** =
[han-gu-geo hal su i-sseo-yo?]

Answer : (네/조금)
[ne] [jo-geum]

Section III - Dictation
Listen to the corresponding MP3 file. Repeat aloud what you hear, then write it down. Each word/phrase will be said twice.

16. Track 48:

17. Track 49:

18. Track 50:

Lesson 18.
To be good/poor at~
잘하다, 못하다

Section I - Vocabulary

Please define/translate each word in English. Then write it in your preferred language.

1. **달리다:**
   [dal-li-da]
   _____

2. **-을/를 못하다:**
   [-eul/reul mo-ta-da]
   _____

3. **노래:**
   [no-rae]
   _____

4. **요리:**
   [yo-ri]
   _____

5. **수영:**
   [su-yeong]
   _____

6. **-을/를 잘하다 :**
   [-eul/reul ja-ra-da]
   _____

7. **맵다:**
   [maep-da]
   _____

8. **풀다:**
   [pul-da]
   _____

9. **퍼즐:**
   [peo-jeul]
   _____

Section II - Comprehension

Fill in the chart - An example has been provided.

Verb (infinitive form)	to be good at "Verb"	to be bad at "Verb"
Ex. 수영하다 [su-yeong-ha-da]	수영을 잘히다 [su-yeong-eul ja-ra-da]	수영을 못하다 [su-yeong-eul mo-ta-da]
10. 일하다 [i-ra-da]		
11. 청소하다 [cheong-so-ha-da]		
12. 공부하다 [gong-bu-ha-da]		
13. 요리하다 [yo-ri-ha-da]		
14. 노래하다 [no-rae-ha-da]		
15. 운동하다 [un-dong-ha-da]		
16. 달리다 [dal-li-da]		
17. 쓰다 [sseu-da]		
18. 먹다 [meok-da]		
19. 마시다 [ma-si-da]		

Section III - Dictation

Listen to the corresponding MP3 file. Repeat aloud what you hear, then write it down. Each word/phrase will be said twice.

20. Track 51:

21. Track 52_ver2:

22. Track 53:

Lesson 19.
Turning Verbs Into Nouns
(nominalization)

Section I - Vocabulary

Fill in the chart – An example has been provided. In the last column, please use your preferred language.

Word	English translation from dictionary	Sentence, word, or image to help me remember
케이크 [ke-i-keu]	cake	I'm going to eat 케이크 for dessert.
1. 보다 [bo-da]		
2. 가다 [ga-da]		
3. 듣다 [deut-da]		
4. 먹다 [meok-da]		
5. 사다 [sa-da]		
6. 만나다 [man-na-da]		

Section II - Comprehension

Turn the verbs from the Vocabulary section into nouns by adding –는 것 and
[-neun geot]
write a definition/translation for each word in English.

1a. _____

2a. _____

3a. _____

4a. _____

5a. _____

6a. _____

Section III - Complete the sentence

Complete the sentence by changing the given verb into a noun and adding the
appropriate particle or sentence ending.

7. 저는 (   ) 좋아해요. (쇼핑하다)
    [jeo-neun (   ) jo-a-hae-yo.]   [syo-ping-ha-da]

8. 제 여자 친구는 아이스크림 (   ) 좋아해요. (먹다)
[je yeo-ja chin-gu-neun a-i-seu-keu-rim (   ) jo-a-hae-yo.]   [meok-da]

9. 지금 (   ) 한국어예요. (공부하다)
[ji-geum (   ) han-gu-geo-ye-yo.]   [gong-bu-ha-da]

10. 제 취미는 책을 (   ). (읽다)
[jc chwi-ⅿl-neun chae-geul (   ).   [ik-tta]

Section IV - Dictation

Listen to the corresponding MP3 file. Repeat aloud what you hear, then write it down. Each word/phrase will be said twice.

11. Track 54:

12. Track 55:

13. Track 56:

Section I – Vocabulary

Match each Korean word to its common English translation.

1. **자다**
   [ja-da]

   a. to buy

2. **쓰다**
   [sseu-da]

   b. to sleep

3. **하다**
   [ha-da]

   c. when

4. **되다**
   [doe-da]

   d. to write

5. **주다**
   [ju-da]

   e. who

6. **사다**
   [sa-dal]

   f. to do

7. **언제**
   [eon-je]

   g. where

8. **누구**
   [nu-gu]

   h. to be done; to be possible

9. **어디**
   [eo-di]

   i. what

10. **뭐**
    [mwo]

    j. to give

Section II - Comprehension
Translate the following sentences into Korean.

11. I have to study today.

    =

12. I have to work.

    =

13. I have to eat.

    =

14. We have to win.
       * to win = 이기다
         [i-gi-da]

    =

15. I should go.

    =

16. Where should I buy the book?

    =

17. Why should I go?

    =

Section III - Dictation
Listen to the corresponding MP3 file. Repeat aloud what you hear, then write it down. Each word/phrase will be said twice.

18. Track 57:

19. Track 58:

20. Track 59:

Lesson 21.
More ~ than ~ ~보다 더

Section I - Vocabulary

Using the given English infinitive, write the Korean adjective with the same meaning using what you know or a Korean dictionary.

1. To be spicy: _____

2. To be big: _____

3. To be healthy: _____

4. To be nice: _____

5. To be fast: _____

6. To be expensive: _____

7. To be difficult: _____

8. To be cold (weather): _____

9. To be hot (weather): _____

10. To be pretty: _____

Section II - Comprehension

Conjugate the words from the Vocabulary section with 더 to create a statement.
Translate the statement to English. [deo]

Ex. 더 맛있어요. = It is more delicious.
[deo ma-si-sseo-yo.]

1a. _____

2a. _____

3a. _____

4a. _____

5a. _____

6a. _____

7a. _____

8a. _____

9a. _____

10a. _____

Section III - Translation practice
Translate the following sentences to Korean.

11. An apple is bigger than a strawberry.

    =

12. My friend is prettier than me.

    =

13. It is colder today than yesterday.

    =

14. Kyeong-eun's cell phone is nicer than Hyunwoo's cell phone.

    =

Section IV - Dictation
Listen to the corresponding MP3 file. Repeat aloud what you hear, then write it down. Each word/phrase will be said twice.

15. Track 60:

16. Track 61:

17. Track 62:

90   *Talk To Me In Korean Workbook*

Lesson 22.
To like 좋다 vs. 좋아하다

Section I - Vocabulary

Please define/translate each word to English. Then write it in your preferred language.

1. **좋다:**
   [jo-ta]
   _____

2. **싫다:**
   [sil-ta]
   _____

3. **싫어하다:**
   [si-reo-ha-da]
   _____

4. **예쁘다:**
   [ye-ppeu-da]
   _____

5. **예뻐하다:**
   [ye-ppeo-ha-da]
   _____

6. **슬프다:**
   [seul-peu-da]
   _____

7. **슬퍼하다:**
   [seul-peo-ha-da]
   _____

8. **영화:**
   [yeong-hwa]
   _____

9. 좋아하다:
    [jo-a-ha-da]
    _____

10. 우유:
    [u-yu]
    _____

11. 드라마:
    [deu-ra-ma]
    _____

12. 비:
    [bi]
    _____

13. 강아지:
    [gang-a-ji]
    _____

Section II - Comprehension

Decide if the statement is true or false. If it is false, correct the underlined term or phrase so that the statement is true.

14. The fundamental difference between 좋아요 and 좋아해요 is that 좋아요
    [jo-a-yo]   [jo-a-hae-yo]   [jo-a-yo]
    means that you like something and 좋아해요 means that something is good.
                                      [jo-a-hae-yo]

        »

15. When you use 좋아요 to say that you like something, such as in, "f(x) 좋아요",
    [jo-a-yo]   [f(x) jo-a-yo]
    the hidden or dropped particle is a subject marking particle.

        »

16. If you want to express, more precisely, that you like something, you can use **좋아요**, which means "to like" or "to be fond of".
[jo-a-yo]

>>

17. If you use the subject marking particle **가**, as in "EXO가 좋아해요", you
[ga]   [EXO-ga jo-a-hae-yo]
need to add what it is that EXO likes because they are the subject of the
sentence.

>>

Section III - Dictation
Listen to the corresponding MP3 file. Repeat aloud what you
hear, then write it down. Each word/phrase will be said twice.

18. Track 63:

19. Track 64:

20. Track 65:

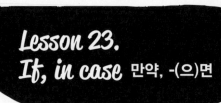

Lesson 23.
If, in case 만약, -(으)면

Section I - Vocabulary

Fill in the chart – An example has been provided. In the last column, please use your preferred language.

Word	Part of speech (noun, verb, adverb, adjective)	English translation from dictionary or TTMIK	Sentence, word, or image to help me remember
케이크 [ke-i-keu]	noun	cake	I'm going to eat 케이크 for dessert.
1. 자다 [ja-da]			
2. 밤 [bam]			
3. 리모콘 [ri-mo-kon]			
4. 작다 [jak-da]			
5. 집 [jip]			
6. 비가 오다 [bi-ga o-da]			
7. 후회하다 [hu-hoe-ha-da]			

Section II - Comprehension

Fill in the chart by conjugating (으)면 with the given verb to make past, present, and future tenses. An example has been provided.

[(eu)myeon]

Verb	English translation	Past Tense	Present Tense	Future Tense
자다 [ja-da]	to sleep	잤으면 [ja-sseu-myeon]	자면 [ja-myeon]	잘 거면 [jal geo-myeon]
8. 보다 [bo-da]				
9. 먹다 [meok-da]				
10. 찾다 [chat-da]				
11. 공부하다 [gong-bu-ha-da]				
12. 오다 [o-da]				
13. 듣다 [deut-da]				
14. 사다 [sa-da]				
15. 하다 [ha-da]				

Section III - Translation practice

Translate each word/phrase to Korean and write it on the line provided.

16. if you sleep now

_____

17. if you saw the movie

_____

18. if you buy it

_____

19. if you are going to watch it

_____

20. If you don't come now, you will regret it.

_____

21. If it rains tomorrow night, I am going to be at home.

_____

Section IV - Dictation

Listen to the corresponding MP3 file. Repeat aloud what you hear, then write it down. Each word/phrase will be said twice.

22. Track 66:

23. Track 67:

24. Track 68:

Lesson 24.
Still, already 아직, 벌써

Section I - Vocabulary
Fill in the blank with the appropriate word from the Word Bank.

Word Bank

왔어요 [wa-sseo-yo]	벌써 [beol-sseo]	to end/finish
모르다 [mo-reu-da]	아직 [a-jik]	아침 [a-chim]
이미 [i-mi]		

1. ( ) means "morning" in Korean.

2. The Korean verb in the infinitive for "to not know" is ( ).

3. "Still" or "not yet" is ( ) in Korean.

4. In 존댓말, the past tense form of 오다 is ( ).
   [jon-daen-mal]   [o-da]

5. (   ) means "already" in Korean.

6. 끝나다 translates to (   ) in English.
    [kkeun-na-da]

7. Another Korean word for "already" is (   ), but
is only used when you and/or the speaker know about something already.

Section II- Comprehension

Short answer – Please respond to the following questions in English. Then write
the answer in your preferred language to help you remember

8. Explain the difference between 아직 and 아직도.
                                    [a-jik]   [a-jik-do]

9. Describe where in a sentence to place the word 벌써.
                                                    [beol-sseo]

10. What is the difference between 이미 and 벌써?
[i-mi]   [beol-sseo]

Section III - Writing

Complete each sentence by choosing either 아직, 벌써, or 이미 to fill in the
[a-jik] [beol-sseo]   [i-mi]
blank.

11. 경은 씨는 (   ) 집에 갔어요.
[gyeong-eun ssi-neun (   ) ji-be ga-sseo-yo.]

= Kyeong-eun already went home. (You have known about this fact since long

before you said this sentence.)

12. 숙제를 (   ) 다 했어요?
[suk-je-reul (   ) da hae-sseo-yo?]

= Have you already done your homework? (Surprised)

13. 현우 씨 (   ) 안 왔어요?
[hyeo-nu ssi (   ) an wa-sseo-yo?]

= Hyunwoo is not here yet?

14. 저는 (   ) 집이에요.
[jeo-neun (   ) ji-bi-e-yo.]

= I am still home.

15. 효진 씨는 (   ) 도착했어요!
[hyo-jin ssi-neun (   ) do-cha-kae-sseo-yo.]

= Hyojin already arrived! (The person you are talking to did not know about this fact before you said it.)

 **Section IV - Dictation**

Listen to the corresponding MP3 file. Repeat aloud what you hear, then write it down. Each word/phrase will be said twice.

16. Track 69:

17. Track 70:

18. Track 71:

Lesson 25. Someone, something, somewhere, someday
누군가, 무언가, 어딘가, 언젠가

Section I - Vocabulary

Match each English word to its equivalent Korean translation.

1. United States

2. To find

3. Somewhere

4. Japan

5. Someday

6. When

7. To go

8. To be strange

9. Something

a. **언젠가**
[eon-jen-ga]

b. **뭔가**
[mwon-ga]

c. **언제**
[eon-je]

d. **어딘가**
[eo-din-ga]

e. **일본**
[il-bon]

f. **이상하다**
[i-sang-ha-da]

g. **찾다**
[chat-da]

h. **미국**
[mi-guk]

i. **가다**
[ga-da]

10. Here, in this place   j. 사다
                                    [sa-da]

11. Someone   k. 중국
                                    [jung-guk]

12. To buy   l. 누군가
                                    [nu-gun-ga]

13. China   m. 여기
                                    [yeo-gi]

Section II - Comprehension

Fill in the blank with the appropriate Korean word to complete each sentence. Then translate each sentence to English and your preferred language.

14. *(something)* (   ) 이상해요.
     [(   ) i-sang-hae-yo.]

     =

15. *(someday)* (   ) 중국어 공부할 거예요.
     [(   ) jung-gu-geo gong-bu-hal geo-ye-yo.]

     =

16. 여기 *(someone)* (   ) 왔어요.
     [yeo-gi (   ) wa-sseo-yo.]

     =

17. 우리 *(somewhere)* (   )에서 만날 거예요.
     [u-ri (   )e-seo man-nal geo-ye-yo.]

     =

Section III - Dictation

Listen to the corresponding MP3 file. Repeat aloud what you hear, then write it down. Each word/phrase will be said twice.

18. Track 72:

19. Track 73:

20. Track 74:

Lesson 26. -(으)세요
Imperative Ending

Section I - Vocabulary

Multiple choice - Circle the best answer.

1. "To sell" in Korean is:

   a. 사다
   [sa-da]

   b. 먹다
   [meok-da]

   c. 접다
   [jeop-da]

   d. 팔다
   [pal-da]

2. 쉬다 means:
   [swi-da]

   a. to rest

   b. to sell

   c. to choose

   d. to fold

3. The Korean word for "hurry up!" is:

   a. 천천히!
   [cheon-cheo-ni!]

   b. 맛있어!
   [ma-si-sseo!]

   c. 대박!
   [dae-bak!]

   d. 빨리!
   [ppal-li!]

4. How do you say "5 o'clock" in Korean?

   a. 세 시
   [se si]

   b. 다섯 시
   [da-seot si]

   c. 경은 씨
   [gyeong-eun ssi]

   d. 한 시
   [han si]

5. What is the Korean word for "to fold"?

   a. 사다
   [sa-da]

   b. 먹다
   [meok-da]

   c. 접다
   [jeop-da]

   d. 팔다
   [pal-da]

6. "To choose" or "to pick" in Korean is:

   a. 사다
   [sa-da]

   b. 고르다
   [go-reu-da]

   c. 접다
   [jeop-da]

   d. 팔다
   [pal-da]

Section II - Comprehension

Translate the following sentences to English and your preferred language (if not English).

7. 이 책을 파세요. =
   [i chae-geul pa-se-yo.]

8. 택시를 타세요. =
   [taek-si-reul ta-se-yo.]

9. 여기에서 기다리세요. =
   [yeo-gi-e-seo gi-da-ri-se-yo.]

10. 한국어 책을 읽으세요. =
    [han-gu-geo chae-geul il-geu-se-yo.]

11. 내일 우리 집에 오세요. =
    [nae-il u-ri ji-be o-se-yo.]

12. TTMIK에서 공부하세요. =
    [TTMIK-e-seo gong-bu-ha-se-yo.]

Section III - Dictation

Listen to the corresponding MP3 file. Repeat aloud what you hear, then write it down. Each word/phrase will be said twice.

13. Track 75:

14. Track 76:

15. Track 77:

Lesson 27.
"Please do something [for me]"
-아/어/여 주세요

Section I - Vocabulary

Please define/translate each word to English. Then write it in your preferred language.

1. **조심하다:**
   [jo-si-ma-da]: _____

2. **돕다:**
   [dop-da]: _____

3. **무섭다:**
   [mu-seop-da]: _____

4. **시작하다:**
   [si-ja-ka-da]: _____

5. **보내다:**
   [bo-nae-da]: _____

6. **일하다:**
   [i-ra-da]: _____

7. **배우다:**
   [bae-u-da]: _____

8. **열다:**
   [yeol-da]: _____

9. **마시다:**
   [ma-si-da]: _____

Section II - Comprehension

Short answer - Please respond to the following questions in English. Then write the answer in your preferred language to help you remember.

10. Explain the main difference between –세요 and –아/어/여 주세요.
    [-se-yo]   [-a/eo/yeo ju-se-yo]

11. Is it more natural to use –세요 or –아/어/여 주세요 when asking for a favor or
    [-se-yo]   [-a/eo/yeo ju-se-yo]
help?

12. What meaning does –세요 take on when you add 주 in order to form –주세요?
    [-se-yo]   [ju]   [-ju-se-yo]

Section III - Writing

Conjugate the given word with either –세요 or –주세요 to create a correct trans-
                              [-se-yo]   [-ju-se-yo]
lation of the statement to Korean.

13. Do it.

* to do = 하다
    [ha-da]

=

Please do me a favor and do it for me.

=

14. Please come.

=

Please do me a favor and come.

=

15. Teach. / Please teach. (to whom is unknown)

=

Please teach me.

=

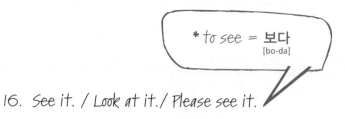

16. See it. / Look at it./ Please see it.

=

Please look at it I'd appreciate it. / Please be kind and see/look at it.

=

17. Buy it. / Please buy it.

* to buy = 사다
[sa-da]

=

Please buy it for me.

=

Section IV - Dictation

Listen to the corresponding MP3 file. Repeat aloud what you hear, then write it down. Each word/phrase will be said twice.

18. Track 78:

19. Track 79:

20. Track 80:

Lesson 28.
Method, way
-(으)로

Section I - Vocabulary

Fill in the blank with an appropriate word from the Word Bank. Not all words are used.

Word Bank

wood	cheese	to speak/talk
to make	road/street	to be famous
left	pen	accident
exit	to get hurt	taxi

1. 만들다 means "(   )" in English.
   [man-deul-da]

2. The word for "(   )" in Korean is 나무.
   [na-mu]

3. "택시 탔어요." = "I took a (   )".
   [taek-si ta-sseo-yo.]

4. "오른쪽" is a directional term which means "right", and "왼쪽" means
   [o-reun-jjok]   [oen-jjok]
   "(   )".

5. "to write with a (   ) " = "펜으로 쓰다"
[pe-neu-ro sseu-da]

6. The Korean word for "(   )" ("치즈") is a loanword, meaning
[chi-jeu]
it's a word borrowed from English and spelled in 한글.
[han-geul]

7. What is the English word for 출구? (   )
[chul-gu]

8. "저는 사고로 다쳤어요." = "I was hurt in an (   )."
[jeo-neun sa-go-ro da-chyeo-sseo-yo.]

9. Audrey Hepburn is considered 유명하다, or "(   )."
[yu-myeong-ha-da]

Section II – Writing practice
Write the following words with the correct particle, either 로 or 으로.
[ro]   [eu-ro]

10. 치즈: ————————
[chi-jeu]

11. 이 길: ————————
[i gil]

12. 친구: ————————
[chin-gu]

13. 2번 출구: ————————
[i-beon chul-gu]

14. **이것:** _____
    [i-geot]

15. **책:** _____
    [chaek]

16. **가방:** _____
    [ga-bang]

17. **회사:** _____
    [hoe-sa]

Section III - Comprehension

Multiple choice - Circle the best answer.

18. −(으)로 has various functions. It can mark:
    [-(eu)-ro]

    a. the ingredients an object is made of

    b. the direction in which someone is going

    c. the status or identity of a person that is doing something

    d. all of the above, plus more.

19. "누가 이 테이블을 나무로 만들었어요." translates to English as:
    [nu-ga i te-i-beu-reul na-mu-ro man-deu-reo-sseo-yo.]

    a. "Who made this tree?"

    b. "Someone made this table with wood."

    c. "To make something with wood."

    d. "I have no clue!"

20. If you are "우리한테 한국어로 말하고 있어요", what are you doing?
[u-ri-han-te han-gu-geo-ro ma-ra-go i-sseo-yo]

    a. Talking to us in Korean

    b. Dreaming of Korean

    c. Telling us about the Korean language

    d. Writing a letter to us in Korean

21. "I will go by taxi." is said how in Korean?

    a. "지하철 타요."
       [ji-ha-cheol ta-yo.]"

    b. "택시 타요."
       [taek-si ta-yo.]"

    c. "버스로 왔어요."
       [beo-seu-ro wa-sseo-yo.]"

    d. "택시로 갈 거예요."
       [taek-si-ro gal geo-ye-yo.]"

Section IV - Dictation

Listen to the corresponding MP3 file. Repeat aloud what you hear, then write it down. Each word/phrase will be said twice.

22. Track 81:

23. Track 82:

24. Track 83:

Lesson 29.
All, more 다, 더

Section I - Vocabulary

Match each English word to its equivalent Korean translation.

1. 준비하다
   [jun-bi-ha-da]

2. 10분
   [sip-bun]

3. 더
   [deo]

4. -(으)면
   [-(eu)-myeon]

5. 다
   [da]

6. 기다리다
   [gi-da-ri-da]

7. 물
   [mul]

8. 주문하다
   [ju-mu-na-da]

9. 피자
   [pi-ja]

10. 커피
    [keo-pi]

a. coffee

b. more

c. all, entirely, whole

d. to wait

e. pizza

f. to order

g. be [get] ready, prepare

h. if

i. 10 minutes

j. water

Section II - Comprehension

True/False - Decide if the statement is true or false. If it is false, correct the underlined term or statement so that the statement is true.

11. In Korean, to say "more", you would use <u>다</u>.
[da]

>>

12. The word 다 seems to act as a noun, but it has a <u>stronger influence on</u>
[da]
<u>verbs than a noun, so you can actually think of it as an adverb.</u>

>>

13. "저는 우유를 더 마셨어요." = "<u>Please give me more milk.</u>"
[jeo-neun u-yu-reul deo ma-syeo-sseo-yo.]

>>

14. 더 influences verbs, such as in "더 사고 싶어요", meaning that you "<u>want to</u>
[deo]   [deo sa-go si-peo-yo]
<u>do more of the buying [action]</u>", rather than wanting to buy more of something.

>>

Section III - Reading comprehension

Read the following journal entry. Unless otherwise noted, all words, sentence endings, and tenses have been covered in TTMIK Levels 1 and 2. Based on what you read, answer the questions below in Korean.

2013-10-26

오늘 친구들이랑 점심으로 피자를 먹었어요. 콜라도 같이 마셨어요. 배가 많이
[o-neul chin-gu-deu-ri-rang jeom-si-meu-ro pi-ja-reul meo-geo-sseo-yo. kol-la-do ga-chi ma-syeo--sseo-yo. bae-ga ma-ni

고팠어요. 그래서 저 혼자 피자 한 판을 다 먹었어요. 그리고 피자를 더 주문했
go-pa-sseo-yo. geu-rae-seo jeo hon-ja pi-ja han pa-neul da meo-geo-sseo-yo. geu-ri-go pi-ja-reul deo ju-mu-nae-sseo-yo. geu-

어요. 그래서 지금 배도 아프고 머리도 아파요.
rae-seo ji-geum bae-do a-peu-go meo-ri-do a-pa-yo.]

* 점심 = lunch
  [jeom-sim]

* 판 = pie (counter for pizza)
  [pan]

15. Who did you go to lunch with?

16. What did you eat?

17. What did you order more of?

18. What body parts hurt?

Section IV - Dictation

Listen to the corresponding MP3 file. Repeat aloud what you hear, then write it down. Each word/phrase will be said twice.

19. Track 84:

20. Track 85:

21. Track 86:

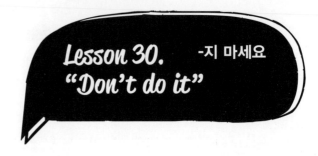

Lesson 30.
"Don't do it"
-지 마세요

Section I - Vocabulary

Please define/translate each word to English. Then write it in your preferred language.

1. 웃다:
   [ut-da]
   _____

2. 말하다:
   [ma-ra-da]
   _____

3. 보내다:
   [bo-nae-da]
   _____

4. 쓰다 *(action verb)*:
   [sseu-da]
   _____

5. 걱정하다:
   [geok-jeong-ha-da]
   _____

6. 만지다:
   [man-ji-da]
   _____

7. 사다:
   [sa-da]
   _____

8. 앉다:
   [an-tta]
   _____

Section II - Fill in the chart: Imperative ending

Conjugate the verbs from the Vocabulary section using the polite imperative form. An example has been provided.

Infinitive (dictionary form)	Please "verb."	Please don't "verb."
Ex. 팔다 [pal-da]	파세요. [pa-se-yo.]	팔지 마세요. [pal-ji ma-se-yo.]
1a.		
2a.		
3a.		
4a.		
5a.		
6a.		
7a.		
8a.		

Section III - Comprehension

Translate the following sentences to Korean and your preferred language (if not English).

9. Please don't eat the entire pizza.

    =

10. Please don't go.

    =

11. Please don't do [that/it].

    =

12. Please don't do the homework.

    =

13. Please don't drink [that/it].

    =

14. Please don't cry.
    * to cry = 울다
              [ul-da]

    =

Section IV - Dictation

Listen to the corresponding MP3 file. Repeat aloud what you hear, then write it down. Each word/phrase will be said twice.

15. Track 87:

16. Track 88:

17. Track 89:

Answer Key
for
TTMIK
Workbook
Level 2

Lesson 1

Section I – Vocabulary

1. to go

2. to do

3. to wear

4. to meet

5. to sell

6. when

7. where

8. now

9. tomorrow

10. how much (money), what price

11. this

12. t-shirt

13. jeans

14. alone (single person)

Section II - Comprehension

15. False - going to do

16. True

17. False - 을 거예요
[eul geo-ye-yo]

18. False - 어디에서 만날 거예요?
[eo-di-e-seo man-nal geo-ye-yo?]

19. True

20. True

Section III - Writing

21. 내일 할 거예요.
[nae-il hal geo-ye-yo.]

22. 삼겹살 먹을 거예요.
[sam-gyeop-sal meo-geul geo-ye-yo.]

23. 5,500원에 팔 거예요.
[o-cheo-no-bae-gwo-ne pal geo-ye-yo.]

Section IV - Dictation

24. 뭐 입을 거예요?
[mwo i-beul geo-ye-yo?]

= What are you going to wear?

25. 누구 만날 거예요?
[nu-gu man-nal geo-ye-yo?]

= Who are you going to meet?

Lesson 2

Section I - Vocabulary

1. noun

   apple

   N/A

2. noun

   television

   N/A

3. noun

   wallet

   N/A

4. adverb

   why

   N/A

5. adjective

   to be strange

   N/A

6. adverb

   often

   N/A

Section II - Writing

7. 밥을
[ba-beul]

8. 오렌지 주스를
[o-ren-ji ju-seu-reul]

9. 그 사람을
[geu sa-ra-meul]

10. 가방을
[ga-bang-eul]

11. 고양이를
[go-yang-i-reul]

12. 학교를
[hak-gyo-reul]

13. 카메라를
[ka-me-ra-reul]

14. 커피를
[keo-pi-reul]

Section III - Comprehension

15. 가
[ga]

16. 를
[reul]

17. 이
[i]

18. 이
[i]

19. 을
[eul]

Section IV - Dictation

20. 어제 뭐 했어요?
[eo-je mwo hae-sseo-yo?]

= What did you do yesterday?

21. 누구를 만났어요?
[nu-gu-reul man-na-sseo-yo?]

= Who did you meet?

22. 지갑 찾았어요?
[ji-gap cha-ja-sseo-yo?]

= Did you find your wallet?

Lesson 3

Section I - Vocabulary

Across	Down
1. kimchi	1. Korean food
5. therefore	2. coffee
8. and	3. student
10. to rain	4. friend
11. house	6. water
12. rice	7. France
13. bread	9. money

Section II - Comprehension

14. d

15. d

16. a

17. d

18. N/A

Section III - Reading comprehension

19. Hyunwoo (현우)
[hyeo-nu]

20. Hyunwoo (현우)
[hyeo-nu]

21. Because the writer didn't have money.

22. coffee shop

23. water

Section IV - Dictation

24. 서울 그리고 부산
[seo-ul geu-ri-go bu-san]

= Seoul and Busan

25. 오늘은 비가 왔어요. 그래서 집에 있었어요.
[o-neu-reun bi-ga wa-sseo-yo. geu-rae-seo ji-be i-sseo-sseo-yo.]

= It rained today. So I was at home.

26. 저는 학생이에요. 그래서 돈이 없어요.
[jeo-neun hak-saeng-i-e-yo. geu-rae-seo do-ni eop-sseo-yo.]

= I am a student. So I don't have money.

Lesson 4

Section I - Vocabulary

1. e

2. i

3. g

4. d

5. f

6. a

7. h

8. c

9. b

10. k

11. j

12. m

13. l

Section II - Comprehension

14. It is a polite way to address someone.

15. If a noun ends in a vowel, you attach 랑
[rang]

at the end, and if it ends with a consonant,

you use 이랑.
[i-rang]

16. 하고 is used like a particle and attached
[ha-go]

right after a noun without a space.

17. 같이 (Write your own sentence that
[ga-chi]

includes 같이)
[ga-chi]

Section III - Dictation

18. 빵이랑 우유
[ppang-i-rang u-yu]

= bread and milk

19. 친구하고 영화 봤어요.
[chin-gu-ha-go yeong-hwa bwa-sseo-yo.]

= I saw a movie with a friend.

20. 누구랑 갔어요?
[nu-gu-rang ga-sseo-yo?]

= Who did you go with/With whom did you go?

Lesson 5

Section I - Vocabulary

1. 토
[to]

2. 언어
[eo-neo]

3. 소풍
[so-pung]

4. 목요일
[mo-gyo-il]

5. 밤
[bam]

6. 영화를 보다
[yeong-hwa-reul bo-da]

7. 화성
[hwa-seong]

8. 목
[mok]

Section II - Comprehension

9. 금요일
[geu-myo-il]

10. 일요일
[i-ryo-il]

11. 수요일
[su-yo-il]

12. 금요일
[geu-myo-il]

13. 토요일
[to-yo-il]

14. 월요일
[wo-ryo-il]

15. 화요일
[hwa-yo-il]

16. 목요일
[mo-gyo-il]

17. 목요일
[mo-gyo-il]

18. 토요일
[to-yo-il]

19. 일요일
[i-ryo-il]

20. 화요일
[hwa-yo-il]

Section III - Dictation

21. 오늘은 금요일이에요.
[o-neu-reun geu-myo-i-ri-e-yo.]

= Today is Friday.

22. 월화수목금토일
[wol-hwa-su-mok-geum-to-il]

23. 토요일에 영화 봤어요.
[to-yo-i-re yeong-hwa bwa-sseo-yo.]

= I watched a movie on Saturday.

Lesson 6

Section I – Vocabulary

1. to be tired

2. movie, film

3. school

4. Sunday

5. to get up

6. every day

7. last night

8. to lose weight

9. late, at a late hour

10. to be perfectly okay

Section II - Writing practice

N/A

Section III - Comprehension

19. 그런데, 그렇지만
[geu-reon-de], [geu-reo-chi-man]

20. 그렇지만
[geu-reo-chi-man]

21. 그런데
[geu-reon-de]

Section IV - Dictation

22. 어제 이거 샀어요. 그런데 정말 커요.
[eo-je i-geo sa-sseo-yo. geu-reon-de jeong-mal keo-yo.]

= I bought this yesterday. And it's really big.

23. 피곤해요. 그렇지만 영화 보고 싶어요.
[pi-go-nae-yo. geu-reo-chi-man yeong-hwa bo-go si-peo-yo.]

= I'm tired. But I want to see a movie.

24. 어제 학교에 갔어요. 그런데 일요일이었어요.
[eo-je hak-gyo-e ga-sseo-yo. geu-reon-de i-ryo-i-ri-eo-sseo-yo.]

= I went to school yesterday. But it was Sunday.

Lesson 7

Section I – Vocabulary

1. d

2. a

3. b

4. d

5. c

Section II - Comprehension

6. False - -에게
[-e-ge]

7. True

8. True

9. False - interchangeable only when they

mean "from [someone]"

10. False - to be beaten by A

Section III - Reading comprehension

11. She had a stomachache.

12. Her friend.

13. She asked for help from people.

14. A middle-aged woman

15. Hospital

Section IV - Dictation

16. 저한테 팔 거예요?
    [jeo-han-te pal geo-ye-yo?]

= Are you going to sell it to me?

17. 친구한테 전화했어요?
    [chin-gu-han-te jeo-nwa-hae-sseo-yo?]

= Did you call your friend?

18. 동생한테 갈 거예요.
    [dong-saeng-han-te gal geo-ye-yo.]

= I will go to my younger brother/sister.

Lesson 8

Section I - Reviewing Korean Numbers

1. f	11. k
2. a	12. l
3. g	13. v
4. b	14. n
5. h	15. p
6. c	16. r
7. i	17. w
8. d	18. t
9. j	19. m
10. e	20. x

21. o

22. q

23. s

24. u

Section II - Comprehension

25. (지금) 여섯 시 십 분이에요.
    [(ji-geum) yeo-seot si sip bu-ni-e-yo.]

26. (지금) 열 시 사십 분이에요.
    [(ji-geum) yeol si sa-sip bu-ni-e-yo.]

27. (지금) 열두 시 이십 분이에요.
    [(ji-geum) yeol-du si i-sip bu-ni-e-yo.]

28. (지금) 두 시 사십오 분이에요.
    [(ji-geum) du si sa-si-bo bu-ni-e-yo.]

29. (지금) 여덟 시 오십칠 분이에요.
    [(ji-geum) yeo-deol si o-sip-chil bu-ni-e-yo.]

30. (지금) 네 시 십구 분이에요.
    [(ji-geum) ne si sip-gu bu-ni-e-yo.]

Section III - Dictation

31. 1:11 (1시 11분)

32. 3:36 (3시 36분)

33. 7:30 (7시 30분)

Lesson 9

Section I - Vocabulary

1. 연필
   [yeon-pil]

2. 돌
   [dol]

3. 공
   [gong]

4. 김치찌개
   [gim-chi-jji-gae]

5. 남다
   [nam-tta]

6. 오리
   [o-ri]

7. 사탕 or 캔디
[sa-tang] [kaen-di]

8. 몇
[myeot]

9. 가방
[ga-bang]

10. 고양이
[go-yang-i]

11. 사과
[sa-gwa]

12. 햄버거
[haem-beo-geo]

13. 커피
[keo-pi]

14. 종이
[jong-i]

15. 사람
[sa-ram]

Section II - Comprehension

16. 명 or 사람
[myeong] [sa-ram]

17. 마리
[ma-ri]

18. 개
[gae]

19. 병
[byeong]

20. 권
[gwon]

21. 장
[jang]

22. 대
[dae]

Section III - Translation Practice

23. 사과 열다섯 개
[sa-gwa yeol-da-seot gae]

24. 고양이 아홉 마리
[go-yang-i a-hop ma-ri]

25. 종이 스물두 장
[jong-i seu-mul-du jang]

26. 책 다섯 권
[chaek da-seot gwon]

27. 연필 서른 자루
[yeon-pil seo-reun ja-ru]

28. 책 한 권 주세요.
[chaek han gwon ju-se-yo.]

29. 개 열한 마리 있어요.
[gae yeo-ran ma-ri i-sseo-yo.]

Section IV - Dictation

30. 사과 스물아홉 개
[sa-gwa seu-mu-ra-hop gae]

= twenty nine apples

31. 사탕 몇 개 있어요?
[sa-tang myeot gae i-sseo-yo?]

= How many candies do you have?

32. 세 개 남았어요.
[se gae na-ma-sseo-yo.]

= There are three left.

Lesson 10

Section I - Vocabulary

1. to do

2. to see

3. to come

4. to buy

5. to listen

6. to rain

7. to study

8. to work

9. to exercise, to work out

10. to sing

Section II - Fill in the chart

1a. 하다
[ha-da]

하고 있어요
[ha-go i-sseo-yo]

하고 있었어요
[ha-go i-sseo-sseo-yo]

하고 있을 거예요
[ha-go i-sseul geo-ye-yo]

2a. 보다
[bo-da]

보고 있어요
[bo-go i-sseo-yo]

보고 있었어요
[bo-go i-sseo-sseo-yo]

보고 있을 거예요
[bo-go i-sseul geo-ye-yo]

3a. 오다
[o-da]

오고 있어요
[o-go i-sseo-yo]

오고 있었어요
[o-go i-sseo-sseo-yo]

오고 있을 거예요
[o-go i-sseul geo-ye-yo]

4a. 사다
[sa-da]

사고 있어요
[sa-go i-sseo-yo]

사고 있었어요
[sa-go i-sseo-sseo-yo]

사고 있을 거예요
[sa-go i-sseul geo-ye-yo]

5a. 듣다
[deut-da]

듣고 있어요
[deut-go i-sseo-yo]

듣고 있었어요
[deut-go i-sseo-sseo-yo]

듣고 있을 거예요
[deut-go i-sseul geo-ye-yo]

6a. 비가 오다
[bi-ga o-da]

비가 오고 있어요
[bi-ga o-go i-sseo-yo]

비가 오고 있었어요
[bi-ga o-go i-sseo-sseo-yo]

비가 오고 있을 거예요
[bi-ga o-go i-sseul geo-ye-yo]

7a. 공부하다
[gong-bu-ha-da]

공부하고 있어요
[gong-bu-ha-go i-sseo-yo]

공부하고 있었어요
[gong-bu-ha-go i-sseo-sseo-yo]

공부하고 있을 거예요
[gong-bu-ha-go i-sseul geo-ye-yo]

8a. 일하다
[i-ra-da]

일하고 있어요
[i-ra-go i-sseo-yo]

일하고 있었어요
[i-ra-go i-sseo-sseo-yo]

일하고 있을 거예요
[i-ra-go i-sseul geo-ye-yo]

9a. 운동하다
[un-dong-ha-da]

운동하고 있어요
[un-dong-ha-go i-sseo-yo]

운동하고 있었어요
[un-dong-ha-go i-sseo-sseo-yo]

운동하고 있을 거예요
[un-dong-ha-go i-sseul geo-ye-yo]

10a. 노래하다
[no-rae-ha-da]

노래하고 있어요
[no-rae-ha-go i-sseo-yo]

노래하고 있었어요
[no-rae-ha-go i-sseo-sseo-yo]

노래하고 있을 거예요
[no-rae-ha-go i-sseul geo-ye-yo]

Section III - Comprehension

11.

1) Literal translation between Korean present progressive sentences and English present progressive sentences does not always work, especially if you use the present progressive form in English to indicate the future.

2) In everyday conversations, sentences that need to be in the present progressive form

do not always take the -고 있어요 form.
[-go i-sseo-yo]
Koreans often just use the plain present tense form even for sentences that take the present progressive tense in English.

Section IV - Dictation

12. 지금 생각하고 있어요.
[ji-geum saeng-ga-ka-go i-sseo-yo.]

= I am thinking now.

13. 졸고 있었어요.
[jol-go i-sseo-sseo-yo.]

= I was dozing.

14. 경은 씨가 자고 있었어요.
[gyeong-eun ssi-ga ja-go i-sseo-sseo-yo.]

= Kyeong-eun was sleeping.

Lesson 11

Section I - Vocabulary

1. swimming

N/A

2. Chinese (language)

N/A

3. name

N/A

4. teacher

N/A

5. USA

N/A

6. bank

N/A

7. younger sister

N/A

8. elementary school student

N/A

9. middle school student, junior high school student

N/A

10. high school student, senior high school student

N/A

11. university student

N/A

12. hobby

N/A

13. age

N/A

14. workplace

N/A

15. job

N/A

16. place of living, residence

N/A

17. family

N/A

18. relatives, extended family

N/A

19. business card

N/A

20. to teach

N/A

21. to be born

N/A

22. to live

N/A

Section II - Comprehension

23. N/A

안녕하세요. 제 이름은 (　　　　　)예요/
[an-nyeong-ha-se-yo.] [je i-reu-meun (　　　)ye-yo/

이에요.
i-e-yo.]

= Hello. My name is (　　　　　).

24. N/A

저는 (　　　)살이에요. 그리고 (
[jeo-neun (　　) sa-ri-e-yo.] [geu-ri-go (

)에 살아요.
)e sa-ra-yo.]

= I am (　　　) years old, and I live in
(　　　　　).

25. N/A

저는 (　　　　　　)예요/이에요.
[jeo-neun (　　　　　)ye-yo/i-e-yo.]

(occupation)

= I am a/an (　　　　　).

26. N/A

그리고 지금 (　　　　　)을/를 공부하고
[geu-ri-go ji-geum (　　　　　)eul/reul gong-bu-ha-go

있어요.
i-sseo-yo.]

= And I am studying (　　　　　) now.

27. N/A

저는 취미가 (　　　　　)예요/이에요.
[jeo-neun chwi-mi-ga (　　　) ye-yo/i-e-yo.]

= My hobby is (　　　　　) .

Section III - Dictation

28. 저는 학생이에요.
[jeo-neun hak-saeng-i-e-yo.]

= I am a student.

29. 저는 서울에 살아요.
[jeo-neun seo-u-re sa-ra-yo.]

= I live in Seoul.

30. 저는 미국에서 태어났어요.
[jeo-neun mi-gu-ge-seo tae-eo-na-sseo-yo.]

= I was born in the USA.

Lesson 12

Section I - Vocabulary

1. k	7. i
2. f	8. a
3. e	9. g
4. l	10. j
5. h	11. c
6. d	12. b

Section II - Comprehension

13. 5월 11일
[o-wol si-bi-ril]

14. 6월, 목요일
[yu-wol]　[mo-gyo-il]

15. 수요일
[su-yo-il]

16. 6월 6일
[yu-wol yu-gil]

17. 금요일 오후 7시, 5월 24일
[geu-myo-il o-hu il-gop si]　[o-wol i-sip-sa-il]

18. 수요일 오전 9시 30분
[su-yo-il o-jeon a-hop si sam-sip bun]

Section III - Dictation

19. 10월 9일 = October 9th
[si-wol gu-il]

20. 6월 30일 = June 30th
[yu-wol sam-si-bil]

21. 생일이 몇 월 며칠이에요? = What date
[saeng-i-ri myeot wol myeo-chi-ri-e-yo?]

is your birthday?/ What is the date of your birthday?

Lesson 13

Section I -Vocabulary

1. c
2. a
3. c
4. b
5. d
6. b
7. d
8. d
9. a
10. c
11. d

Section II - Comprehension

12. topic marking particle
13. particles
14. 반말
    [ban-mal]
15. can change
16. "Please give some water to me, too."
17. "Please also give some water to me."

Section III - Translation Practice

18. I am a student, too.
19. This is also a pencil.
20. That person is studying, too.
21. I also want to go to China.

22. My head also hurts.

23. Ma'am~! Please give me a bottle of cola here. And please give me a bottle of Sprite, too.

Section IV - Dictation

24. 저도 갈 거예요.
    [jeo-do gal geo-ye-yo.]

= I will go, too.

25. 오늘도 일해요?
    [o-neul-do i-rae-yo?]

= Do you work today as well?

26. 이것도 가져왔어요.
    [i-geot-do ga-jyeo-wa-sseo-yo.]

= I brought this, too.

Lesson 14

Section I - Vocabulary

1. English
2. to teach
3. computer
4. to fix
5. to catch
6. to sell
7. to buy
8. to eat
9. to see

Section II - Comprehension

10. True

11. False - "to do + the verb in the noun form + also"

12. True

13. False - can just separate the noun part of the verb from 하다 and add -도 after the noun part

14. True

15. True

Section III- Dictation

16. 영화를 보기도 해요.
[yeong-hwa-reul bo-gi-do hae-yo.]

= I also watch movies. / I even watch movies.

17. 잠을 자기도 해요.
[ja-meul ja-gi-do hae-yo.]

= I also sleep. / I even sleep.

18. 제가 청소도 할 거예요.
[je-ga cheong-so-do hal geo-ye-yo.]

= I will also do the cleaning.

Lesson 15

Section I - Vocabulary

1. b

2. c

3. a

4. c

5. d

6. b

7. a

8. c

9. b

Section II - Comprehension

10. 주기만 하다
[ju-gi-man ha-da]

to only give

11. 일 년만
[il nyeon-man]

only one year

12. 가르치기만 하다
[ga-reu-chi-gi-man ha-da]

to only teach

13. 살기만 하다
[sal-gi-man ha-da]

to only live

14. 소리만
[so-ri-man]

only sound

15. 여자만
[yeo-ja-man]

only women

16. 돈만
[don-man]

only money

17. 소녀시대만
[so-nyeo-si-dae-man]

only Girls' Generation

18. 읽기만 하다
[il-kki-man ha-da]

to only read

19. 열기만 하다
[yeol-gi-man ha-da]

to only open

20. 웃기만 하다
[ut-gi-man ha-da]

to only laugh

Section III- Dictation

21. 이것만 주세요.
[i-geot-man ju-se-yo.]

= Please give me only this.

22. 보기만 할 거예요.
[bo-gi-man hal geo-ye-yo.]

= I will only look (and not touch it).

23. 책 한 권만 주문했어요
[chaek han gwon-man ju-mu-nae-sseo-yo.]

= I only ordered one book.

Lesson 16

Section I - Vocabulary

1. a little, a bit, a little bit

2. to be expensive

3. to be fast

4. to be strange

5. really, truly

6. really, truly - the same meaning as 정말,
[jeong-mal]

but a little less formal than 정말
[jeong-mal]

7. very, quite

8. to be delicious

9. to be far away

10. to be interesting; to be fun

11. to be bad

12. not at all - only used with negative sentences

13. to be busy

14. to be hot

Section II - Comprehension

15. 아주 is the most standard way of saying
[a-ju]

"very" in the written form, but more often

than not, in spoken Korean, 아주 is often
[a-ju]

replaced with 정말 or 진짜.
[jeong-mal] [jin-jja]

16. When you are referring to the meaning of

"quite" or "very", you can also use the word,

조금, based on the assumption that the other
[jo-geum]

person understands what you mean. For ex

ample, if you say "조금 비싸요," it can mean
[jo-geum bi-ssa-yo]

either "it's a little bit expensive" or "it's quite

expensive".

17. When 조금 is pronounced quickly, it often
[jo-geum]

becomes 좀 (often pronounced like 쯈), and is
[jom]   [jjom]

frequently written this way, as well.

18. 조금, 아주, and 정말 can be used with any
[jo-geum] [a-ju]   [jeong-mal]

sentence, but 별로 and 전혀 can only be used
[byeol-lo]   [jeo-nyeo]

with negative sentences.

Section III - Translation practice

19. 조금 비싸요.
[jo-geum bi-ssa-yo.]

20. 별로 안 비싸요.
[byeol-lo an bi-ssa-yo.]

21. 현우 씨는 정말/진짜/아주 이상해요.
[hyeo-nu ssi-neun jeong-mal/jin-jja/a-ju i-sang-hae-yo.]

or 현우 씨가 정말/진짜/아주 이상해요.
[hyeo-nu ssi-ga jeong-mal/jin-jja/a-ju i-sang-hae-yo.]

22. 이 오렌지는 정말/진짜/아주 맛있어요.
[i o-ren-ji-neun jeong-mal/jin-jja/a-ju ma-si-sseo-yo.]

or 이 오렌지가 정말/진짜/아주 맛있어요.
[i o-ren-ji-ga jeong-mal/jin-jja/a-ju ma-si-sseo-yo.]

Section IV- Dictation

23. 조금만 주세요.
[jo-geum-man ju-se-yo.]

= Give me only a little bit.

24. 별로 재미없어요.
[byeol-lo jae-mi-eop-sseo-yo.]

= It's not that interesting.

25. 전혀 안 바빠요.
[jeo-nyeo an ba-ppa-yo.]

= I'm not busy at all.

Lesson 17

Section I - Vocabulary

Across	Down
2. do	1. go
5. Japanese	2. drive
8. can	3. read
9. sleep	4. cannot
11. meet	6. exist
	7. see
	10. eat

Section II - Comprehension

12. Can we meet tomorrow?

네. 만날 수 있어요.
[ne. man-nal su i-sseo-yo.]

13. Can you read this book?

아니요. 못 읽어요.
[a-ni-yo. mot il-geo-yo.]

14. Can you make tteokbokki?

아니요. 못 만들어요.
[a-ni-yo. mot man-deu-reo-yo.]

15. Can you speak Korean?

네. 조금 할 수 있어요.
[ne. jo-geum hal su i-sseo-yo.]

Section III- Dictation

16. 이거 먹을 수 있어요?
[i-geo meo-geul su i-sseo-yo?]

= Can you eat this?

17. 오늘 일찍 잘 수 있어요?
[o-neul il-jjik jal su i-sseo-yo?]

 = Can you go to bed early today?

18. 그거 못 먹어요.
[geu-geo mot meo-geo-yo.]

= I can't eat it.

Lesson 18

Section I - Vocabulary

1. to run

2. to be poor at

3. singing; song

4. cooking, dish

5. swimming

6. to be good at

7. to be spicy

8. to solve

9. puzzle/puzzles

Section II - Comprehension

10. 일을 잘하다
[i-reul ja-ra-da]

일을 못하다
[i-reul mo-ta-da]

11. 청소를 잘하다
[cheong-so-reul ja-ra-da]

청소를 못하다
[cheong-so-reul mo-ta-da]

12. 공부를 잘하다
[gong-bu-reul ja-ra-da]

공부를 못하다
[gong-bu-reul mo-ta-da]

13. 요리를 잘하다
[yo-ri-reul ja-ra-da]

요리를 못하다
[yo-ri-reul mo-ta-da]

14. 노래를 잘하다
[no-rae-reul ja-ra-da]

노래를 못하다
[no-rae-reul mo-ta-da]

15. 운동을 잘하다
[un-dong-eul ja-ra-da]

운동을 못하다
[un-dong-eul mo-ta-da]

16. 잘 달리다
[jal dal-li-da]

못 달리다
[mot dal-li-da]

17. 잘 쓰다
[jal sseu-da]

못 쓰다
[mot sseu-da]

18. 잘 먹다
[jal meok-da]

못 먹다
[mot meok-da]

19. 잘 마시다
[jal ma-si-da]

못 마시다
[mot ma-si-da]

Section III - Dictation

20. 제 친구는 노래를 잘해요.
[je chin-gu-neun no-rae-reul ja-rae-yo.]

= My friend is good at singing. / My friend

can sing.

21. 경은 씨는 요리 잘해요?
[gyeong-eun ssi-neun yo-ri ja-rae-yo?]

= Are you a good cook, Kyeong-eun? /

Are you good at cooking, Kyeong-eun?

22. 효진 씨 글씨 잘 써요.
[hyo-jin ssi geul-ssi jal sseo-yo.]

= Hyojin is good at handwriting.

Lesson 19

Section I - Vocabulary

1. to see

N/A

2. to go

N/A

3. to listen

N/A

4. to eat

N/A

5. to buy

N/A

6. to meet

N/A

Section II - Comprehension

1a. 보는 것
[bo-naeun geot]

= seeing; the act of seeing; the thing that you

see; what you watch

2a. 가는 것 = going; the act of going
[ga-neun geot]

3a. 듣는 것= listening; the act of listening; the
[deun-neun geot]

thing that you listen; what you listen

4a. 먹는 것 = eating; the act of eating; the
[meong-neun geot]

thing that you eat; what you eat

5a. 사는 것 = buying; the act of buying; the
[sa-neun geot]

thing that you buy; what you buy

6a. 만나는 것 = the act of meeting; the fact
[man-na-neun geot]

that you meet

Section III - Complete the sentence

7. 쇼핑하는 것을
[syo-ping-ha-neun geo-seul]

8. 먹는 것을
[meong-neun geo-seul]

9. 공부하는 것은
[gong-bu-ha-neun geo-seun]

or 공부하는 것이
[gong-bu-ha-neun geo-si]

10. 읽는 것이에요.
[ing-neun geo-si-e-yo.]

or 읽는 거예요.
[ing-neun geo-ye-yo.]

Section IV - Dictation

11. 한국어 공부하는 거 힘들어요?
[han-gu-geo gong-bu-ha-neun geo him-deu-reo-yo?]

= Is studying Korean tough?/ Is it hard to

study Korean?

12. 뭐 하는 거 좋아해요?
[mwo ha-neun geo jo-a-hae-yo?]

= What do you like to do?

13. 일하는 거 재미있어요?
[i-ra-neun geo jae-mi-i-sseo-yo?]

= Is working fun?

Lesson 20

Section I - Vocabulary

1. b	6. a
2. d	7. c
3. f	8. e
4. h	9. g
5. j	10. i

Section II - Comprehension

11. 오늘 공부해야 해요/돼요.
[o-neul gong-bu-hae-ya hae-yo/dwae-yo.]

12. 일해야 해요/돼요.
[i-rae-ya hae-yo/dwae-yo.]

13. 먹어야 해요/돼요.
[meo-geo-ya hae-yo/dwae-yo.]

14. 이겨야 해요/돼요.
[i-gyeo-ya hae-yo/dwae-yo.]

15. 가야 해요/돼요.
[ga-ya hae-yo/dwae-yo.]

16. 그 책 어디에서 사야 해요/돼요?
[geu chaek eo-di-e-seo sa-ya hae-yo/dwae-yo?]

17. 저 왜 가야 해요/돼요?
[jeo wae ga-ya hae-yo/dwae-yo?]

Section III - Dictation

18. 이거 언제까지 해야 돼요?
[i-geo eon-je-kka-ji hae-ya dwae-yo?]

= Until when should I do this? / Until when

should I finish this?/ When do I need to finish

this?

19. 집에 가야 돼요.
[ji-be ga-ya dwae-yo.]

= I have to go home.

20. 누구한테 말해야 돼요?
[nu-gu-han-te ma-rae-ya dwae-yo?]

= Who should I talk to?/ To whom should I

speak?

Lesson 21

Section I - Vocabulary

1. 맵다
[maep-da]

2. 크다
[keu-da]

3. 건강하다
[geon-gang-ha-da]

4. 좋다
[jo-ta]

5. 빠르다
[ppa-reu-da]

6. 비싸다
[bi-ssa-da]

7. 어렵다
[eo-ryeop-da]

8. 춥다
[chup-da]

9. 덥다
[deop-da]

10. 예쁘다
[ye-ppeu-da]

Section II - Comprehension

1a. 더 매워요. = It is spicier.
[deo mae-wo-yo.]

2a. 더 커요. = It is bigger.
[deo keo-yo.]

3a. 더 건강해요. = It is healthier.
[deo geon-gang-hae-yo.]

4a. 더 좋아요. = It is nicer.
[deo jo-a-yo.]

5a. 더 빨라요. = It is faster.
[deo ppal-la-yo.]

6a. 더 비싸요. = It is more expensive.
[deo bi-ssa-yo.]

7a. 더 어려워요. = It is more difficult.
[deo eo-ryeo-wo-yo.]

8a. 더 추워요. = It is colder.
[deo chu-wo-yo.]

9a. 더 더워요. = It is hotter.
[deo deo-wo-yo.]

10a. 더 예뻐요. = It is prettier.
[deo ye-ppeo-yo.]

Section III - Translation practice

11. 사과는 딸기보다 (더) 커요.
[sa-gwa-neun ttal-gi-bo-da (deo) keo-yo.]

12. 제 친구는 저보다 (더) 예뻐요.
[je chin-gu-neun jeo-bo-da (deo) ye-ppeo-yo.]

13. 오늘은 어제보다 (더) 추워요.
[o-neu-reun eo-je-bo-da (deo) chu-wo-yo.]

14. 경은 씨 핸드폰이 현우 씨 핸드폰보다
[gyeong-eun ssi haen-deu-po-ni hyeo-nu ssi haen-deu-pon-bo-da

(더) 좋아요.
(deo) jo-a-yo.]

Section IV - Dictation

15. 이것보다 저것이 더 좋아요.
[i-geot-bo-da jeo-geo-si deo jo-a-yo.]

= I like that one more than this one.

/ That one is nicer than this one.

16. 누가 더 빨라요?
[nu-ga deo ppal-la-yo?]

= Who is faster?

17. 저는 먹는 것보다 자는 것을 더
[jeo-neun meong-neun geot-bo-da ja-neun geo-seul deo

좋아해요.
jo-a-hae-yo.]

= I like sleeping more than eating.

Lesson 22

Section I - Vocabulary

1. to be good

2. to be unlikable; to be undesirable

3. to hate, to not like

4. to be pretty; to be cute

5. to consider someone pretty and treat

them in such a manner

6. to be sad

7. to feel sad and therefore express such emotions

8. movie, film

9. to like, to be fond of; to enjoy doing something

10. milk

11. soap opera, TV show, drama

12. rain

13. puppy

Section II - Comprehension

14. False - 좋아요 means that something
[jo-a-yo]

is good and 좋아해요 means that you like
[jo-a-hae-yo]

something.

15. True

16. False - 좋아해요
[jo-a-hae-yo]

17. True

Section III - Dictation

18. 저는 우유 안 좋아해요.
[jeo-neun u-yu an jo-a-hae-yo.]

= I don't like milk.

19. 슬퍼하지 마세요.
[seul-peo-ha-ji ma-se-yo.]

= Don't be sad.

20. 뭐가 제일 좋아요?
[mwo-ga je-il jo-a-yo?]

= What is your favorite?

Lesson 23

Section I - Vocabulary

1. verb

to sleep

N/A

2. noun

night

N/A

3. noun

remote control

N/A

4. adjective

to be small

N/A

5. noun

house, home

N/A

6. verb

to rain

N/A

7. verb

to regret

N/A

Section II - Comprehension

8. to see, to watch

봤으면
[bwa-sseu-myeon]

보면
[bo-myeon]

볼 거면
[bol geo-myeon]

9. to eat

먹었으면
[meo-geo-sseu-myeon]

먹으면
[meo-geu-myeon]

먹을 거면
[meo-geul geo-myeon]

10. to find

찾았으면
[cha-ja-sseu-myeon]

찾으면
[cha-jeu-myeon]

찾을 거면
[cha-jeul geo-myeon]

11. to study

공부했으면
[gong-bu-hae-sseu-myeon]

공부하면
[gong-bu-ha-myeon]

공부할 거면
[gong-bu-hal geo-myeon]

12. to come

왔으면
[wa-sseu-myeon]

오면
[o-myeon]

올 거면
[ol geo-myeon]

13. to hear, to listen

들었으면
[deu-reo-sseu-myeon]

들으면
[deu-reu-myeon]

들을 거면
[deu-reul geo-myeon]

14. to buy

샀으면
[sa-sseu-myeon]

사면
[sa-myeon]

살 거면
[sal geo-myeon]

15. to do

했으면
[hae-sseu-myeon]

하면
[ha-myeon]

할 거면
[hal geo-myeon]

Section III - Translation practice

16. 지금 자면
[ji-geum ja-myeon]

17. 그 영화 봤으면
[geu yeong-hwa bwa-sseu-myeon]

18. (그거) 사면
[(geu-geo) sa-myeon]

19. (그거) 볼 거면
[(geu-geo) bol geo-myeon]

20. 지금 안 오면, 후회할 거예요.
[ji-geum an o-myeon, hu-hoe-hal geo-ye-yo.]

21. 내일 밤에 비가 오면, 집에 있을 거예요.
[nae-il ba-me bi-ga o-myeon, ji-be i-sseul geo-ye-yo.]

Section IV - Dictation

22. 리모콘 찾으면 저 주세요.
[ri-mo-kon cha-jeu-myeon jeo ju-se-yo.]

= If you find the remote control, please give

it to me.

23. 이거 먹으면 배가 아플 거예요.
[i-geo meo-geu-myeon bae-ga a-peul geo-ye-yo.]

= If you eat this, you will have a stomachache.

24. 공부 많이 했으면 어렵지 않을 거예요.
[gong-bu ma-ni hae-sseu-myeon eo-ryeop-ji a-neul geo-ye-yo.]

= If you studied a lot, it will not be difficult.

Lesson 24

Section I - Vocabulary

1. 아침
[a-chim]

2. 모르다
[mo-reu-da]

3. 아직
[a-jik]

4. 왔어요
[wa-sseo-yo]

5. 벌써
[beol-sseo]

6. to end/finish

7. 이미
[i-mi]

Section II- Comprehension

8. 아직도 emphasizes the meaning of "still
[a-jik-do]
happening" or "still not happening", and has

a meaning of criticizing the other person or

being a little bit mad or angry about what's

still happening or not happening.

9. 벌써 is generally placed at the beginning of
[beol-sseo]
sentences, but it doesn't always have to be at

the beginning.

10. When you and/or the speaker know

about something already and talk about it,

you use 이미. When you are just finding out
[i-mi]
about something as you speak, you use 벌써.
[beol-sseo]
People don't always stick to this rule, but this

is the basic idea.

Section III - Writing

11. 이미
[i-mi]

12. 벌써
[beol-sseo]

13. 아직
[a-jik]

14. 아직
[a-jik]

15. 벌써
[beol-sseo]

Section IV - Dictation

16. 벌써 끝났어요?
[beol-sseo kkeun-na-sseo-yo?]

= Is it already over?

17. 학교는 이미 졸업했어요.
[hak-gyo-neun i-mi jo-reo-pae-sseo-yo.]

= I already graduated from school.

18. 왜 아직 안 갔어요?
[wae a-jik an ga-sseo-yo?]

= Why are you still here?

Lesson 25

Section I - Vocabulary

1. h

2. g

3. d

4. e

5. a

6. c

7. i

8. f

9. b

10. m

11. l

12. j

13. k

Section II - Comprehension

14. 뭔가 - Something is strange.
[mwon-ga]

15. 언젠가 - I will study Chinese someday.
[eon-jen-ga]

16. 누군가 - Someone came here.
[nu-gun-ga]

17. 어딘가 - We are going to meet some-
[eo-din-ga]

where.

Section III - Dictation

18. 언젠가는 말할 거예요.
[eon-jen-ga-neun ma-ral geo-ye-yo.]

= Someday I will say it./ I will tell someday.

19. 어딘가에 있을 거예요.
[eo-din-ga-e i-sseul geo-ye-yo.]

= It must be somewhere.

20. 뭔가 달라요.
[mwon-ga dal-la-yo.]

= Something is different.

Lesson 26

Section I - Vocabulary

1. d

2. a

3. d

4. b

5. c

6. b

Section II - Comprehension

7. Please sell this book.

8. Please take a taxi.

9. Please wait here.

10. Please read Korean books.

11. Please come to my house tomorrow.

12. Please study at TTMIK.

Section III - Dictation

13. 내일 네 시에 오세요.
[nae-il ne si-e o-se-yo.]

= Please come here at four o'clock tomorrow.

14. 그거 저한테 파세요.
[geu-geo jeo-han-te pa-se-yo.]

= Please sell it to me.

15. 여기서 기다리세요.
[yeo-gi-seo gi-da-ri-se-yo.]

= Please wait here.

Lesson 27

Section I - Vocabulary

1. to be careful

2. to help

3. to be scary, to be scared

4. to begin, to start

5. to send

6. to work

7. to learn

8. to open

9. to drink

Section II - Comprehension

10. Instead of just adding -(으)세요 after the
[-(eu)se-yo]

verb stem, if you add -아/어/여 주세요, the sen-
[-a/eo/yeo ju-se-yo]

tences have a nuance of asking for a favor

or asking the other person to do something for

you.

11. -아/어/여 주세요
[-a/eo/yeo ju-se-yo]

12. 주세요 comes from 주다, which means
[ju-se-yo]   [ju-da]

"to give." By adding 주세요 after a verb, you
[ju-se-yo]

add the meaning of "give me [the act of]"

doing something, so it means "do it for me".

Section III - Writing

13. 하세요. , 해 주세요.
[ha-se-yo.]   [hae ju-se-yo.]

14. 오세요. , 와 주세요.
[o-se-yo.]   [wa ju-se-yo.]

15. 가르치세요. , 가르쳐 주세요.
[ga-reu-chi-se-yo.] [ga-reu-chyeo ju-se-yo.]

16. 보세요. , 봐 주세요.
[bo-se-yo.] [bwa ju-se-yo.]

17. 사세요. , 사 주세요.
[sa-se-yo.] [sa ju-se-yo.]

Section III - Dictation

18. 지금 시작해 주세요.
[ji-geum si-ja-kae ju-se-yo.]

= Please be kind and start now.

19. 책 읽어 주세요.
[chaek il-geo ju-se-yo.]

= Please read a book to me.

20. 저한테 보내 주세요.
[jeo-han-te bo-nae ju-se-yo.]

= Please send it to me.

Lesson 28

Section I - Vocabulary

1. to make

2. wood

3. taxi

4. left

5. pen

6. cheese

7. exit

8. accident

9. to be famous

Section II - Writing practice

10. 치즈로
[chi-jeu-ro]

11. 이 길로
[i gil-lo]

12. 친구로
[chin-gu-ro]

13. 2번 출구로
[i-beon chul-gu-ro]

14. 이것으로
[i-geo-seu-ro]

15. 책으로
[chae-geu-ro]

16. 가방으로
[ga-bang-eu-ro]

17. 회사로
[hoe-sa-ro]

Section III - Comprehension

18. d   20. a

19. b   21. d

Section IV - Dictation

22. 이거 뭐로 만들었어요?
[i-geo mwo-ro man-deu-reo-sseo-yo?]

= What did you make this with? / What is

this made of?

23. 오른쪽으로 가세요.
[o-reun-jjo-geu-ro ga-se-yo.]

= Please go to the right. / Please go through the right side.

24. 한 손으로 들 수 있어요?
[han so-neu-ro deul su i-sseo-yo?]

= Can you hold it with one hand?

Lesson 29

Section I - Vocabulary

1. g
2. i
3. b
4. h
5. c
6. d
7. j
8. f
9. e
10. a

Section II - Comprehension

11. False - 더
[deo]
12. True
13. False - I drank more milk.
14. True

Section III - Reading comprehension

15. 친구들
[chin-gu-deul]
16. 피자, 콜라
[pi-ja] [kol-la]
17. 피자
[pi-ja]
18. 배, 머리
[bae] [meo-ri]

Section IV - Dictation

19. 조금만 더 기다려 주세요.
[jo-geum-man deo gi-da-ryeo ju-se-yo.]

= Please wait only a little more (a little longer).

20. 벌써 다 했어요?
[beol-sseo da hae-sseo-yo?]

= Have you already done [it]?

21. 다 사고 싶어요.
[da sa-go si-peo-yo.]

= I want to buy all [this].

Lesson 30

Section I - Vocabulary

1. to laugh, to smile
2. to tell, to say, to talk, to speak
3. to send
4. to write; to use
5. to worry
6. to touch
7. to buy
8. to sit

Section II - Fill in the chart: Imperative ending

1a. 웃다.
[ut-da.]

웃으세요.
[u-seu-se-yo.]

웃지 마세요.
[ut-ji ma-se-yo.]

2a. 말하다.
[ma-ra-da.]

말하세요.
[ma-ra-se-yo.]

말하지 마세요.
[ma-ra-ji ma-se-yo.]

3a. 보내다.
[bo-nae-da.]

보내세요.
[bo-nae-se-yo.]

보내지 마세요.
[bo-nae-ji ma-se-yo.]

4a. 쓰다.
[sseu-da.]

쓰세요.
[sseu-se-yo.]

쓰지 마세요.
[sseu-ji ma-se-yo.]

5a. 걱정하다.
[geok-jeong-ha-da.]

걱정하세요.
[geok-jeong-ha-se-yo.]

걱정하지 마세요.
[geok-jeong-ha-ji ma-se-yo.]

6a. 만지다.
[man-ji-da.]

만지세요.
[man-ji-se-yo.]

만지지 마세요.
[man-ji-ji ma-se-yo.]

7a. 사다.
[sa-da.]

사세요.
[sa-se-yo.]

사지 마세요.
[sa-ji ma-se-yo.]

8a. 앉다.
[an-da.]

앉으세요.
[an-jeu-se-yo.]

앉지 마세요.
[an-jji ma-se-yo.]

Section III - Comprehension

9. 피자 다 먹지 마세요.
[pi-ja da meok-ji ma-se-yo.]

10. 가지 마세요.
[ga-ji ma-se-yo.]

11. 하지 마세요.
[ha-ji ma-se-yo.]

12. 숙제 하지 마세요.
[suk-je ha-ji ma-se-yo.]

13. 마시지 마세요.
[ma-si-ji ma-se-yo.]

14. 울지 마세요.
[ul-ji ma-se-yo.]

Section III - Dictation

15. 아직 시작하지 마세요.
[a-jik si-ja-ka-ji ma-se-yo.]

= Don't start yet.

16. 저한테 전화하지 마세요.
[jeo-han-te jeo-nwa-ha-ji ma-se-yo.]

= Don't call me.

17. 혼자 집에 가지 마세요.
[hon-ja ji-be ga-ji ma-se-yo.]

= Don't go home alone.